Floral
DIMENSIONS

20 STUNNING 3D FLOWERS TO MACHINE APPLIQUE

Floral
DIMENSIONS

PAULINE
INESON

David and Charles
www.rucraft.co.uk

Contents

12

18

22

26

56

92

62

74

32

96

66

78

38

102

70

82

42

106

50

86

112

Introduction

Flowers are perennial favourites in patchwork, appliqué and quilting and this book shows you how to create twenty irresistible fabric flowers in wonderful three-dimension. A delightful range of blooms is described, a veritable garden in fact, from pretty little marigolds and intricate fuchsias to stately foxgloves and elegant tulips. Some of the flowers are very realistic while others are more representational but all are very rewarding to make.

A wide variety of techniques are used to make the flowers, including ruching fabric, gathering and coiling fabric and, of course, many appliqué techniques. All of the flowers are explained with step-by-step instructions, clear diagrams and inspiring photographs and there are also instructions for making stems and various leaf shapes.

Suggestions are included throughout on the fabrics and colours you might use, with stitched variations shown to inspire you. Advice is also given on how the flowers might be used in a quilt block, with detailed photographs of the blocks from my Floral Dimensions Quilt (see overleaf). Of course, any of the flowers would be perfect to use in smaller projects too, such as bags, wall hangings and household decorations. The flowers are presented in alphabetical order, with the templates required at the end of each chapter. General techniques needed are covered in a section at the back of the book.

So come into my three-dimensional flower garden and start with your favourite flower. Soon you will have a beautiful bouquet of flowers to adorn all sorts of lovely sewing projects.

To download full-size printable PDFs of the templates go to:
www.jellyrollquilters.com/page/templates.

FLORAL DIMENSION QUILT

The flowers in this book are all the dimensional ones I used on my award-winning quilt, 'Floral Dimensions', shown opposite. Having made my Heirloom Quilt, which included over thirty-six sewing machine techniques, I then set out to make a quilt that incorporated as many machine sewn appliqué techniques as I could find.

I started with reverse appliqué and added Hawaiian and Celtic designs. When I began making some of the dimensional flowers I enjoyed the challenge so much that the quilt took a different direction and eventually I discarded the reverse appliqué block and substituted it for a more dimensional cyclamen design. I tried to make most of the flowers to look like the real thing but others, mostly the ones used as single centre flowers on the blocks, I named after they were made so you have to stretch your imagination a little!

I entered the quilt in Quilts UK 2010 at Malvern where it won Best Bed Quilt, Best Sampler Quilt and Visitors Choice Award. It then went on to win First Place in the Traditional Quilts category in the Festival of Quilts show at the National Exhibition Centre in Birmingham in 2010. I was also thrilled to receive Second Place for a First Entry in an AQS Show, in Paducah, Kentucky, USA in 2011 and an Honourable Mention in the 2011 International Quilt Show at Houston, USA.

If the three-dimensional flowers in this book inspire you and you would like to incorporate them into a large quilt, then you can obtain the patterns for each of the blocks for the quilt from my website. As well as the flower-themed blocks, patterns are also available for the trapunto, Celtic and Hawaiian blocks and the borders. The patterns describe how to complete the quilt using my quilt-as-you-go-back-to-front technique. For all patterns go to: www.paulineineson.co.uk

Materials and Equipment

The flowers in this book only require small amounts of fabric, sometimes just scraps really, so you will probably have plenty to choose from in your fabric stash. Fusible web will also be needed, plus a few other materials, such as stabilizer, to make sewing easier. Various items of equipment are suggested, although you may have your own favourites.

FABRICS

Quilting cotton and silk are probably the best fabrics to use, finer rather than thicker and not too loosely woven. There really is no limit on colour choice. If you want your flowers to look realistic, then batiks work very well. You could go to the other extreme and choose bold stripes and prints or totally different colourways from the real thing. I chose something in between, using pinks, yellows and greens with a few patterned fabrics which I 'fussy cut'. Fussy cutting is great fun – picking out small motifs for a particular part of the flower. You do, however, end up with very holey fabric!

STABILIZER

A tear-away stabilizer is really useful to provide a stable base for machine stitching and will help when sewing stitches such as satin stitch. I have occasionally used a water-soluble stabilizer called Solvy, mainly for when I satin stitched a raw edge with no background fabric. This stabilizer tears away and any surplus can be removed with a wet cotton bud, leaving a clean edge. Make sure you don't buy the thicker version (Ultra Solvy) as this will not rip away from the stitching.

FUSIBLE INTERFACING

When making the flowers I used a medium-weight fusible interfacing occasionally as a backing for shapes that are stitched around the edge and turned through to the right side by making a slit in the interfacing. A lightweight one is too flimsy and may rip apart when you turn the shape through.

FUSIBLE WEB

For appliqué I use Steam-A-Seam 2 but you could use Bondaweb (also called Wonder Under and Vliesofix). The instructions describe using Steam-A-Seam, which has a paper backing on each side. Bondaweb only has a paper backing on one side, so consult the product instructions. I've used Steam-A-Seam as a base for turning raw edges to the wrong side and in these cases Bondaweb is not a suitable substitute as the paper backing is not firm enough. See Using Fusible Web in the General Techniques section.

SEAM SEALANT

Some of the flowers benefit from sealing the seams to prevent fraying and a product such as Fray Check works well for this.

FABRIC MARKERS

When fabric needs to be marked, an air-erasable fabric marker is useful as it fades after a time. You could use another, easily removed marker. Always test markers on your intended fabrics.

SEWING MACHINE

You will only need a basic machine to make the flowers. I have only used a few stitches – a straight stitch, zigzag, satin and blind hem stitch. The minimum you will need, apart from a straight stitch, is a zigzag that can have the length and width adjusted. This can be used as a substitute for the blind hem stitch and satin stitch (which is only a squished-up zigzag!).

WADDING (BATTING)

Small amounts of quilt wadding (batting) are needed for some of the flowers and leaves. Scraps and small offcuts will be fine.

THICK WOOL (YARN)

A soft wool yarn, similar to that used in trapunto work, is needed to stuff flower stems.

NEEDLES AND THREADS

A Universal 70 machine needle is the best for most of the sewing. I do like to use a 70 Sharp needle for satin stitching. A blunt hand-sewing needle with a large eye is useful for stuffing stems.

For threads I used mainly polyester weight 50, top and bobbin, to match the colour of the fabric for the straight sewing. I used a rayon thread, weight 40 on the top, with either the same in the bobbin or bobbin thread (depending on where the stitching will be) for the satin stitching. A cotton thread for both of these stitches would work fine. Thicker threads for sewing tendrils are also needed – about the thickness of six-stranded embroidery threads. See also Needles and Threads for Appliqué in the General Techniques section.

OTHER ITEMS

These small items of equipment are all optional but do make life a little easier!

- Bias bars – these are also called bias press bars and are useful for making the bias tubes needed for some flower stems.
- Template plastic – this thin plastic is excellent for creating templates and being transparent allows you to fussy cut fabrics easily.
- Set of Mylar circles – Mylar is a heat-resistant plastic, so is very useful when fabric needs to be pressed with a template still in place. Circles in various diameters can be bought as a set.
- Needle gripper – this is a pair of small ribbed forceps that are useful for turning small shapes through to the right side and also for stuffing small shapes.
- Point turner – this little gadget helps to turn points out so they are sharp. Some brands act as seam creasers too.
- Fabric folding pen – when a line is drawn with this special pen it makes fabric pliable and easy to crease.
- Embroidery hoop – this is useful for some of the flowers, to hold the fabric taut, especially when machine satin stitching.
- Toy stuffing – very small amounts of toy stuffing are required for filling some flowers.
- Spray starch – this is useful for firming up fabrics and creating a firm crease when ironing.
- Seed beads – some of the flowers are enhanced by the addition of tiny beads at the ends of stamens.
- Glue stick – special glue sticks are available for fabrics, such as the Sewline brand.

Begonia

The begonia is a pretty little flower that grows in a wide range of colours in tightly ruffled petals. I used delicate creams and pinks and chose to 'fussy cut' my fabric for the two petals, so that a different motif was seen in the centre of the small petals compared to the large ones. You may choose to do something similar or select two different shades for the small and large petals. The templates provided make the petal formation easy.

REQUIREMENTS
- Background fabric, size according to your quilt block or project
- Fabric for the stem, begonia petals and begonia centre
- Machine sewing thread, cotton or polyester, to match fabrics
- Small strip of fusible web
- Soft wool (yarn) to stuff the stem

Making the Stem

1 Cut a 1in x 3in (2.5cm x 7.6cm) bias strip for the begonia stem. Refer to Making Bias Stems in the General Techniques section to make the stem and blind hem stitch it in place – see Blind Hem Stitching Appliqué. Stuff the stem with wool.

Making the Flower Centre

2 Cut a ½in x 6in (1.3cm x 15.2cm) bias strip from your chosen fabric and cut both ends at a 45 degree angle. With the wrong side (WS) facing up, sew a gathering stitch down the centre of the length of the strip (machine stitch length 3.5, and loosen the tension), securing the stitches at the beginning but not at the end (see Fig 1).

3 Trim the thread tails that have been secured at the beginning and then pull up the bobbin thread that is on the right side of the strip, so it measures about 2in (5.1cm). Knot the thread tails but do not cut them. Beginning at the end that has the cut thread tails, roll the strip so the wrong side is on the inside (Fig 2). Thread a needle with the thread tails and use this to sew the end to the roll. Push the needle through the centre of the roll a few times in different places to secure it.

Fig 1

Fig 2

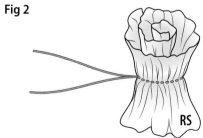

Making the Petals

4 When choosing your fabrics for the petals, you may want to use two shades, one for the smaller petals and one for the larger petals, in which case, you won't need Template 2 and will need to *omit* steps 6 and 7 below. If you plan to fussy cut the fabrics (that is, select specific motifs from your fabric for the petals), then you will be using both Templates 1 and 2 and should *omit* step 5.

The begonia has five small petals in the centre and five larger ones underneath, around the outside. The template for the petals is a kidney shape, one end smaller than the other (see end of this chapter for the templates). This kidney shape is cut out in fabric and sewn to another piece of fabric resulting in a double-sided shape (Fig 3A). The smaller end on one side of the petal shape is for the centre petals and the larger end on the other side of the petal shape is for the petals underneath (Fig 3B and 3C).

6 Make a template of Templates 1 and 2 from template plastic. On the right side of the fabric you are using for the small petals, position Template 2 so the smaller end of the shape is over your chosen motif (Fig 4). Draw around the template and then repeat this four times. Using the same template, draw around it five times on the right side of the fabric you are using for the large petals, positioning your chosen motif under the larger end of the shape each time (Fig 5). Cut out the shapes on the line.

Fig 4

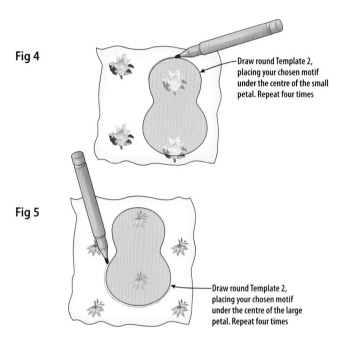

Draw round Template 2, placing your chosen motif under the centre of the small petal. Repeat four times

Fig 5

Draw round Template 2, placing your chosen motif under the centre of the large petal. Repeat four times

Fig 3A

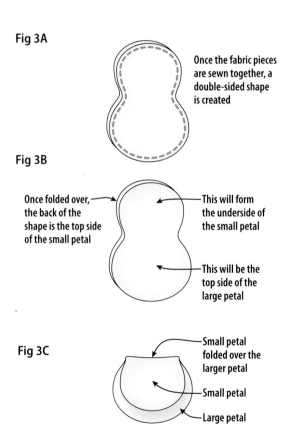

Once the fabric pieces are sewn together, a double-sided shape is created

Fig 3B

Once folded over, the back of the shape is the top side of the small petal

This will form the underside of the small petal

This will be the top side of the large petal

Fig 3C

Small petal folded over the larger petal

Small petal

Large petal

7 Place one of each of the two different fabrics, right sides together, forming five pairs. Make sure that when you put them together the motifs are at opposite ends. On each of the pairs, place Template 1 on top in the centre, draw around it and then sew on the line (Fig 6).

Fig 6

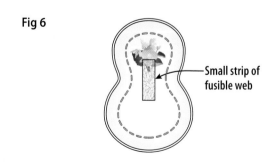

Small strip of fusible web

5 Make a copy of Template 1 on to template plastic – refer to Copying a Template in General Techniques. Place the fabric for the small petals on top of the fabric you are using for the large petals, right sides together and draw around the petal shape five times, leaving about ½in (1.3cm) space between them. Sew on the line around each shape and cut them out about ⅛in (3mm) away from the stitching.

Tip When sewing around a small shape that is to be turned through, shorten the stitch length to 1.5.

8 On the wrong side iron a thin strip of fusible web just above the middle on the side being used for the small petal. Turn the shape over and make a small slit, about ⅜in (1cm) long, on the fabric used for the large petal, not too near to the large petal end (Fig 7). Clip the seam allowance to the stitching line at the 'waist' on either side. Peel off the backing paper from the web, turn each shape through to the right side and iron flat, bringing the raw edges of the slit together and fusing them over the web underneath.

Fig 7

9 Overlap five petals, slit side up, in a row with ¼in (6mm) showing between each of them (Fig 8A). Use fabric glue or pin in place. Draw a line across the 'waists' of the shapes and then machine a straight stitch along the line, leaving thread tails and securing both ends (Fig 8B).

Fig 8

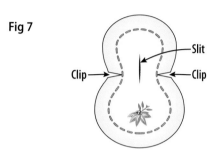

10 Turn the strip of petals over to the front (the side without slits) and place a begonia centre made earlier, in the middle. Thread a needle and knot the end. Bring the needle up from the centre of the back of the petal strip, through to the front and then through the centre roll. Put the needle back in the petal strip about ½in (1.3cm) away from where it came up, moving the centre roll over to meet the petal strip (Fig 9). Bring the needle to the back of the strip again and sew a few stitches close together to secure.

Fig 9

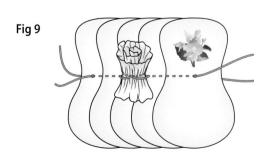

11 Roll the petal strip around the centre, overlapping the first and last petal by ¼in (6mm) (see Tip below). Hand sew to secure, pushing the needle through the centre and out the other side. Take one stitch towards you and push the needle back through the centre again. Repeat this process until the centre is secure.

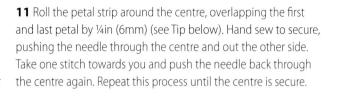

Tip

If your petal strip isn't long enough to go around the centre and overlap the first petal, then you will need to adjust the width of your strip. Similarly, if it's too long, then make your original petal strip a little shorter. It all depends on the thickness of your fabric!

12 Turn the small petals over the large petals. Sew the edges of the centre petals to the large petals that are underneath. Fluff up the centres on the front of the flower and then hand sew the back of the centre to the back of the large petals to keep the flower flat. To finish, hand sew the flowers to the background fabric by catching the underneath of each large petal. See Making Leaves for ideas on leaves to accompany this flower.

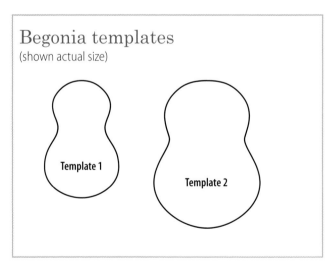

Begonia templates
(shown actual size)

Template 1

Template 2

Design Inspirations...

Made by Geraldine Clarke

Made by Sallie Hopper

The petal formation in the begonia flower is double-sided, which gives opportunities for choosing contrasting colours or prints for the petals. Alternatively, you could choose one fabric for the inner petals and another for the larger outer petals. Two examples are shown here to inspire you.

The block in my quilt that features the begonia has a single marigold in the centre with eight begonia flowers arranged in a circular design around it. Pairs and clusters of leaves fill in the design and also hide the ends of the marigold stems. Crosshatch quilting across the background fabric is all that is needed to complete the block.

Bell flower

Little flowers in the shape of bells are quite simple to create and this shape can be the basis for many flowers, creating a wonderful three-dimensional quality. These simple bells are also perfect for decorating with tiny seed beads and a line of delicate pearls has been sewn inside the bell. The flowers are made by sewing two fabric pieces together and then turning through to the right side and could easily be made larger if you desire.

REQUIREMENTS
- Background fabric, size according to your quilt block or project
- Fabric for flower, about 3in (7.6cm) square
- Machine sewing thread to match the fabric
- Fusible web
- Tear-away stabilizer
- Seven small beads ⅛in (3mm) diameter

Making the Bell

1 Using the template supplied at the end of the chapter, draw around the shape for the bell on to the wrong side of your fabric, placing the arrow on the template on the straight grain. Place a piece of the same fabric under the piece you have drawn the shape on, right sides together. Sew a straight stitch, length 1.5 on the line but not along the bottom edge. Cut out the shape to within about ⅛in (3mm) of the sewing line. Mark the fold line and then cut a V shape out of the seam allowance at the fold line (see Fig 1). Finger press or iron the seams as open as possible.

2 Draw around the fusible web pattern twice on the smooth side (paper side) of a piece of fusible web and cut the shapes out on the line. Iron one shape to the lower part of the sewn shapes on each side and then peel off the backing paper (Fig 2).

3 If the shape is turned through at this stage, then the folded edge along the bottom of the bell will have pointy sides at the seams. To eliminate this, a dart needs to be sewn at each side before the shape is turned through. To do this, push the bottom half of the bell up to the inside of the top half at the fold line, right sides together. Sew a small dart at the folded edge on both sides where the seams are (Fig 3). This dart should be very shallow and only needs to round off the point at the seam. Place tear-away stabilizer underneath before you sew and tear it away afterwards.

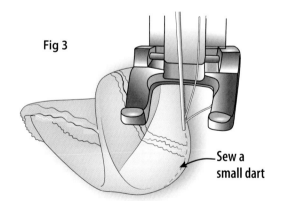

Fig 3

Sew a small dart

4 Turn the shape to the right side through the gap at the base. Push the lower half into the top half, wrong sides together, pushing the raw edge to the inside of the top half and then creasing along the fold line. Iron the inside of the bell using a mini iron or just the point of a regular iron, so that the fusible web sticks the two layers together.

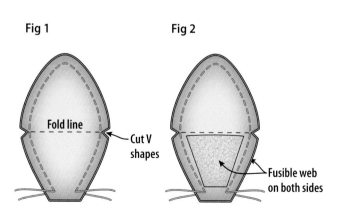

Fig 1

Fold line

Cut V shapes

Fig 2

Fusible web on both sides

Adding the Beads

5 Thread a small bead in the centre of a 9in (23cm) length of thread (Fig 4A) and tie a double knot next to the bead to secure it (Fig 4B). Bring the two thread ends together and thread them through a needle. Thread six more beads on the threads (Fig 4C). Attach the line of beads to the inside of the bell, at the top, bringing the needle out to the back of the bell and then securing the thread with a few stitches sewn on top of each other.

Fig 4A   **Fig 4B**   **Fig 4C**

Knot

Knot

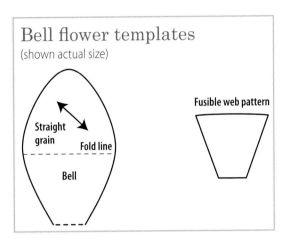

Bell flower templates
(shown actual size)

Straight grain

Fold line

Bell

Fusible web pattern

Design Inspirations...

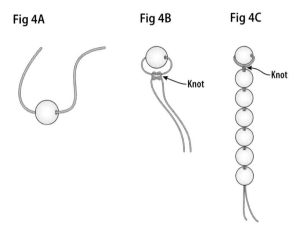

Made by Sallie Hopper

Made by Sandra Pirie

These little bell flowers add a charming touch to a design and can be made in any colours you like. They are very useful to add a touch of brighter accent colour if you feel a block needs a bit more emphasis. The colour of the beads can blend with the fabric colour or contrast with it.

The block in my quilt is a roundel, composed of pansies, bell flowers and a lily. The pansies and bell flowers are mirror images at the sides of the design, with a pink lily at the top and a cluster of leaves at the base.

Berries and Grapes

A bunch of plump grapes or a cluster of juicy berries is a lovely three-dimensional motif to add to a quilt block. You could make the tightly stuffed round shapes as individual additions or as a little trio, as shown in the block in the Cyclamen chapter. If you are making a bunch of grapes or berries, then you might want to vary the fabric shades to make them look more realistic.

REQUIREMENTS
- Background fabric, size according to your quilt block or project
- Fabric for each berry or grape about 2in (5.1cm) square
- Fabric for leaves 6in x 4in (15.2cm x 10.2cm)
- Machine sewing thread to match the fabric and rayon or polyester thread for leaf machine satin stitching
- Heatproof plastic template (Mylar) 1in (2.5cm) diameter or use a suitable coin
- Small amount of toy stuffing
- Wadding (batting) for leaves
- Fusible web for leaves

Making a Grape or Berry

1 On the wrong side of the fabric, draw a circle 1in (2.5cm) in diameter using a template or a coin. Sew a machine gathering stitch (length 3.0) on the line leaving thread tails at the beginning and end. Tie the threads that are on the wrong side together with a triple knot and trim them to about 1in (2.5cm) – see Fig 1A.

2 Turn the fabric so the right side is on top and cut about ¼in (6mm) from the line, making sure you don't cut off the thread tails. Pull up the thread tails on the right side a little and stuff the shape quite tightly with stuffing to eliminate any little pleats that may form on the edges (Fig 1B). Now pull the threads up again as tightly as you can, knot them together and use the thread tails to sew across the opening a few times (Fig 1C).

Fig 1A

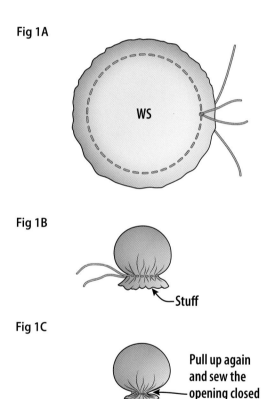

WS

Fig 1B

Stuff

Fig 1C

Pull up again
and sew the
opening closed

> **Tip** To make stuffing the small shapes a easier, instead of using a stick, use a pair of tweezers to grip the stuffing and push it in at the same time. Even better, use a pair of needle grippers as these aren't as sharp as tweezers and the blades are ridged, which will grip the stuffing better.

Attaching to the Background Fabric

3 Hand sewing a bunch of grapes to a background can be a little tricky as they need to fit snugly against the fabric. One of my ladies, Avril Hann, came up with this way. She drew all the circles on to the fabric in a pattern as a bunch, leaving about ¼in (6mm) between them. She then sewed the gathering stitches as shown in Fig 2, pulled them up and stuffed them as above and then cut the fabric around the outside of the bunch. The grapes were then sewn on to the background as a bunch by turning under the raw edges that are on the outside of the bunch. A few stab stitches are needed to keep the bunch flat.

Fig 2

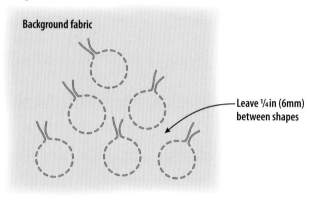

Background fabric

Leave ¼in (6mm)
between shapes

> **Tip** If you want to vary your fabrics, you could sew the grapes or berries in groups or strips of three or four, using a different fabric each time.

Making Leaves

4 The grapes look more realistic with leaves but are optional if you prefer. Trace the leaf shapes on a piece of fusible web (I used Steam-A-Seam), on the backing paper that has the web attached, and then roughly cut them out. Peel off the backing paper that was not drawn on and iron the leaf shapes to the wrong side of the fabric. Cut the leaves out on the line.

5 Peel off the second backing paper and place the leaves in position on the background fabric. Satin stitch, width 2.0, using a matching thread – see Satin Stitching.

6 Pin a piece of wadding (batting) under each leaf on the wrong side of the background fabric and triple stitch the vein lines, length 3.0. Sew a straight stitch next to the satin stitching on the inside only. Trim the wadding on the back close to the straight stitching.

Grape leaves templates
(shown actual size)

Design Inspirations...

Made by Sandra Pirie

Made by Sallie Hopper

The technique for making these lovely plump globes is very simple and you are sure to find lots of ways to use them in your quiltmaking. They look very effective in a grouping of just three and even more impressive as a whole bunch. Grading your fabric colours will make them look even more lifelike, as these examples show.

In my quilt block I've used two large bunches, including some grape leaves and curling tendrils for further realism. A lily of the valley flower was added for visual balance.

Carnation

Whether you like grand florist's carnations or pretty garden pinks, the frilly edges of this flower are very distinctive and rewarding to create in fabric. Pink is a favourite colour but try white, lemon or red. To make my carnation flower I used two fabrics fused wrong sides together and then edged the petals with an irregular machine satin stitch. You could use two slightly different shades for added interest. Try using a contrasting thread around the edges.

REQUIREMENTS
- Background fabric, size according to your quilt block or project
- Fabric for the stem, calyx, leaves and petals
- Machine sewing thread, cotton or polyester, to match fabrics
- Rayon, polyester or cotton thread for satin stitch edging
- Fusible web
- Water-soluble stabilizer
- Cord or wool to stuff stem
- Toy stuffing for calyx
- Seam sealant liquid (optional)
- Embroidery hoop (optional)

Making the Leaves

1 Cut a bias strip from your leaf fabric about 2in x 4in (5cm x 10.2cm) and a 2in (5.1cm) square of fusible web (I used Steam-A-Seam). Iron the fusible web (remove one of the backing papers first if using Steam-A-Seam) on to one half of the wrong side of the fabric – see Fig 1A. Peel the backing paper from the web, fold over the other half of the fabric and iron. You will now have two layers of fabric with the wrong sides stuck together (Fig 1B).

Fig 1A

Fig 1B

2 Using the templates at the end of this chapter, draw around the carnation leaf shape twice on the double layer of fabric using an easily removable marker. Cut the leaves out on the line.

3 Thread your machine with the same thread on top and in the bobbin – preferably a rayon thread. Select a satin stitch, width 2.0–2.5, and adjust the tension so that the top and underneath look the same. You may have to tighten the tension slightly (a higher number) if your machine sets the stitch automatically (refer to Satin Stitching in the General Techniques section). Sandwich the leaves between two layers of water-soluble stabilizer (I used Solvy). Satin stitch around the edges of the leaves so that the left swing of the needle goes into the fabric and the right swing goes just off the edge. Remove the stabilizer. A drop of a seam sealant such as Fray Check can be applied to the tips of the leaves to prevent any stitches from dropping off the end.

Tip

When working the machine satin stitch you may find it easier to put the stabilizer sandwich in a hoop and use a metal or Teflon foot rather than a plastic one. You could use tear-away stabilizer but this can leave a white edge where it has been torn away. You may be able to sew the edge without a stabilizer, so experiment first.

4 Pin the leaves in position (refer to the template for placement). The base of the leaves should meet at the centre of where the stem will be sewn. Zigzag these two edges together but do not sew any more of the leaves at this point.

Making the Stem

5 Cut a 1in x 2½in (2.5cm x 6.3cm) bias strip (or your chosen length). Refer to Making Bias Stems in the General Techniques section to make the stem. Blind hem stitch the stem to the background fabric, over the join of the two leaves (see Blind Hem Stitching Appliqué). Stuff the stem with wool. Bring the points of the leaves down and hand sew in place.

Making the Calyx

6 Trace the calyx template on to the wrong side of the calyx fabric and cut it out. Fold where indicated by the dotted lines on the template, wrong sides facing, mitring the corners at the top and making the bottom edge the same width as the stem. Place the calyx over the stem, just above the top leaf (refer to the template for placement). Blind hem stitch the two sides and bottom. Push a little stuffing in through the top and then blind hem stitch the top edge closed.

Making the Petals

7 Draw three 1⅝in (4.1cm) diameter circles on the fusible web and roughly cut them out (Fig 2A). In the centre of each circle draw another circle 1¼in (3.2cm) diameter and cut it out. You will now have a fusible web doughnut (Fig 2B).

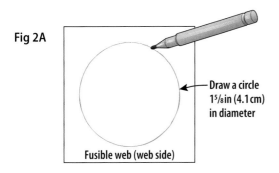

Fig 2A

Draw a circle 1⅝in (4.1cm) in diameter

Fusible web (web side)

Fig 2B

Hole

Draw an inner circle 1¼in (3.2cm) in diameter and cut it out

8 Peel off the backing paper without the line on and iron the shapes to the wrong side of the petal fabric. Cut the fabric and fusible web on the outside line only (Fig 3). Peel off the second backing paper and iron the shape on to another piece of the same fabric, wrong sides facing. Cut the second fabric level with the edge of the first one (Fig 4).

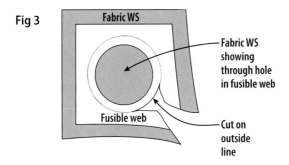

Fig 3

Fabric WS

Fabric WS showing through hole in fusible web

Fusible web

Cut on outside line

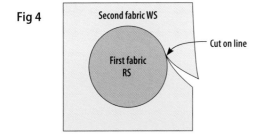

Fig 4

Second fabric WS

First fabric RS

Cut on line

9 Thread your machine with the same thread on top and in the bobbin – preferably a rayon. Select a satin stitch (or satin stitch with an irregular edge if you have one – see Fig 5), width 3.0–4 and adjust the tension so the top and underneath look the same. Sew along the edge of each circle so the left swing of the needle goes into the fabric and the right swing goes just off the edge. You may be able to do this without stabilizer as it won't matter if the edge isn't exactly even. If this doesn't work, use stabilizer as for the leaves.

10 On the right side, draw a ¾in (2cm) diameter circle in the centre of each circle and machine sew a gathering stitch, length 4.0, on the line. Leave thread tails but do not secure the beginning or end. Tie the threads on the right side and bury them. Pull up the threads on the other side tightly to gather the centre of the circle (see Fig 6). Knot and bury the ends.

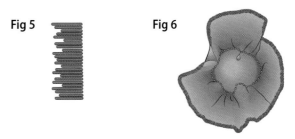

Fig 5

Fig 6

11 Using a removable marker, draw the three carnation placement circles from the placement guide template on to the background fabric. Hand sew one carnation flower to the centre of each of these circles. Catch a few of the carnation petals to the background and a few of them to each other at the edges to form a flower.

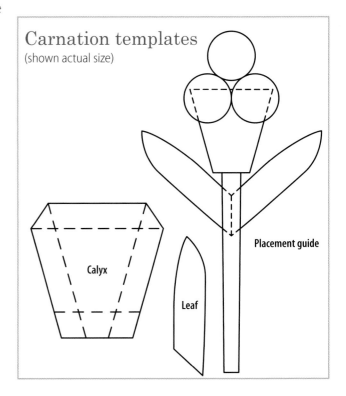

Carnation templates
(shown actual size)

Placement guide

Calyx

Leaf

Design Inspirations...

Made by Sandra Pirie

Made by Sallie Hopper

Carnations or pinks are such lovely flowers. Pink is a favourite colour of course and there are so many shades to choose from, ranging from delicate blush pink to sizzling cerise, or you could use red or purple for a more dramatic look. The examples shown here use a satin stitch edging in a thread that tones with the petal fabric but try a contrasting thread colour for a bolder picot look.

For the block in my quilt I used carnation flowers with daffodils, around a central gazania flower. The flowers really take centre stage in the block, with small leaves for colour contrast.

Chrysanthemum

Chrysanthemums come in all shapes, sizes and colours, from tight little pompons to hugely decorative mop heads. The chrysanthemum flower I've created here is really two flowers in one. The outer section is a scrunched and ruched flower, with a smaller picot-edged blossom in the centre. You really can make the flower in any colour you like, and using a different colour in the centre is very effective. The main technique used is simple ruching and gathering of the fabric.

REQUIREMENTS
- Background fabric, size according to your quilt block or project
- Fabric, about 6in (15.2cm) square for the outer flower and 2in (5.1cm) square for the inner one
- Heatproof template plastic (Mylar) 4in (10.2cm) diameter circle
- Regular template plastic 4in (10.2cm) diameter circle
- Fusible web
- Wadding (batting)
- Machine sewing thread to match fabric

Making the Outer Flower

1 Cut out a 4in (10.2cm) diameter circle in heatproof template plastic. On the fabric wrong side draw around the circle and cut out about ¾in (2cm) from the line (Fig 1). Sew a gathering stitch a little outside the line (stitch length 3.5, with a slightly lower tension). Do not secure the stitches at either end. Place the circle template on the wrong side of the fabric in the middle and pull up the bobbin threads to gather the edge around the circle. Iron the edge flat, remove the template and iron again (Fig 2).

2 Trace the ruching guide on to template plastic and cut it out on the line. Place the template on top of the right side of the fabric and mark around the zigzag edge using a removable marking pen or pencil. Machine a gathering stitch (as in step 1) all around the edge along the zigzag line (Fig 3). Use the needle down position if you have one, to make it easier to pivot at the points. Knot the thread ends that are on the right side, sew them through to the back and trim to about 1in (2.5cm) long.

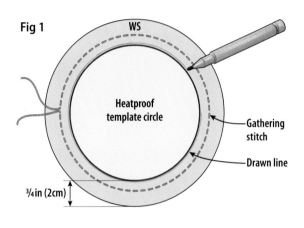

Fig 1

WS

Heatproof template circle

Gathering stitch

Drawn line

¾in (2cm)

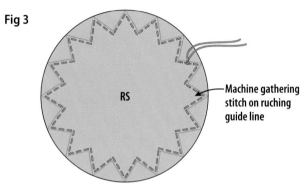

Fig 3

RS

Machine gathering stitch on ruching guide line

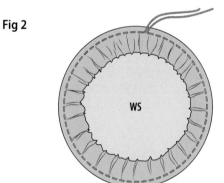

Fig 2

WS

3 Using a straight stitch, length 4 and lowered tension, sew four lines across the flower (Fig 4). Leave thread tails at the beginning and end and be careful not to sew on the previous line of stitches. Pull up the thread tails that are on the wrong side of the outer row of stitching until the circle measures just under 3in (7.6cm) across. Knot and trim the ends. Adjust the scallops around the edge so they are even. Pull up the thread tails from the four lines of stitching crossing the flower, until the inside of the circle is reasonably flat and scrunched.

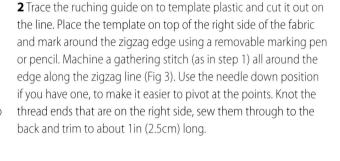

When sewing gathering stitches use a polyester thread in the machine as it is stronger than cotton or rayon. If you use a different shade in the top and bobbin it is easier to determine which thread to pull up – the bobbin one is the easiest. When knotting the top threads before pulling up, use a triple knot as a double one may work loose.

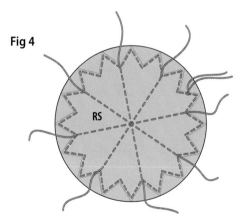

Fig 4

RS

4 Cut out a 2½in (6.3cm) diameter circle of fusible web. Peel off the backing paper from one side (if using Steam-A-Seam) and place this, web side down, on to the wrong side of the flower. Scrunch the centre of the flower and pin around the edge. Press lightly. Remove the four lines of gathering stitches and re-press. Remove the backing paper from the fusible web.

5 Cut a 2½in (6.3cm) diameter circle of wadding and pin it beneath the flower. Sew the flower to the background with a straight stitch all around the inside of the scallop edge (Fig 5).

Fig 5

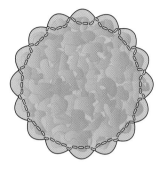

Making the Picot-Edged Flower

6 On the wrong side of the fabric you are using for the flower centre, draw a 1¼in (3.2cm) diameter circle. Sew a gathering stitch on the line (length 3.5, tension lowered). Knot the threads that are on the wrong side and cut them off about 1in (2.5cm) away from the knot. Trim the fabric about ⅜in (1cm) from the stitching, making sure you don't cut off the thread tails.

7 Place a 1in (2.5cm) diameter heatproof template circle in the centre of the wrong side of the fabric. Pull up the thread tails that are on the right side. Knot the tails and pull through to the wrong side. Iron the edge flat. Remove the template and then iron again.

8 On the right side, sew a picot stitch around the edge (see Fig 6 for example of this stitch). Use the regular machine foot for this, shorten the length and tighten the tension. The right swing of the stitch should go over the edge of the circle and the straight stitches in the fabric. You may have to adjust the length and width of the stitch so that you are sewing small scallops around the edge of the flower.

Fig 6

9 To finish, sew the small flower on top of the scrunched outer flower around the inner line of the picot stitch (Fig 7).

Fig 7

When stitching the picot edge, practise first by folding a scrap of fabric along the bias and ironing flat. Sew the picot edge along the folded edge, adjusting the width, length and tension as necessary.

Chrysanthemum template
(shown actual size)

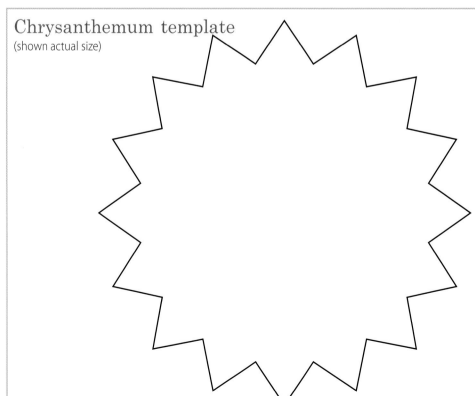

Design Inspirations...

Made by Sallie Hopper

Made by Katherine Willis

Making chrysanthemum flowers is great fun as they aren't meant to be totally realistic so you can feel free to do your own thing. The variations here also show how you can change the colour to suit your quilt block.

My quilt block placed a chrysanthemum flower in the centre of the block, accompanied by four tulips and four clematis flowers. I chose a greenish fabric for the chrysanthemum, to link it with the stems and leaves of the other flowers.

Clematis

The clematis flower is very simple to make and has an interesting frayed centre, which represents the boss of stamens in the centre of a real clematis flower. Clematis flowers often have a vein of colour up through each petal and you could reflect this in your fabric colour choices. The petals are in two groups of three and can be made using two different shades of fabric. The tendrils are added with machine chain stitch.

REQUIREMENTS
- Background fabric, size according to your quilt block or project
- Fabric for stem, bias strip 1in x 5in (2.5cm x 12.7cm)
- Fabric for petals about 4in x 6in (10.2cm x 15.2cm)
- Fabric for frayed centre, two 1¼in (3.2cm) squares
- Machine sewing thread, cotton or polyester, to match fabrics
- Thin decorative cord or embroidery thread for tendrils
- Fusible web
- Wool (yarn) for stuffing the stem
- Seam sealant liquid
- Easily removable fabric marker

Making the Stems

1 Cut a bias strip 1in x 5in (2.5cm x 12.7cm) and make the stem – refer to Making Bias Stems in the General Techniques section. Blind hem stitch the stem in place on your background fabric – refer to Blind Hem Stitching Appliqué. Stuff the stem with one strand of soft wool (yarn).

Adding the Tendrils

2 The tendrils are completed before the flower so the flower petals can hide the ends of the tendrils. Using the thin cord and a machine chain stitch method, sew three tendrils to the background fabric (see photos). See Creating Tendrils in General Techniques.

Making the Flower

3 Using the template provided at the end of this chapter, draw around the clematis petal shape twice on your fusible web (I used Steam-A-Seam). Cut them out on the line. Peel the backing off one of the backing papers from each shape (if using Steam-A-Seam). Stick the shapes to the wrong side of the petal fabric. Cut the fabric about ¼in (6mm) from the edge of the fusible web. Put a drop of seam sealant at each inward curve near the centre.

4 Make three small slits at each inward curve near the centre, right up to the edge of the template – see Fig 1. Turn the fabric over the edges of the fusible web – refer to step 3 of Turning Raw Edges to the Wrong Side. As you go, check the front of the petals to make sure you are keeping the curves smooth.

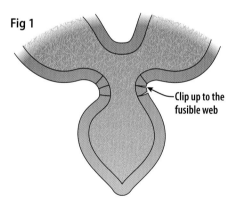

Fig 1

Clip up to the fusible web

5 Remove the fusible web backing paper from one petal at a time and press the edges back down before removing the backing paper from the centre.

6 Iron one three-petal shape in place on your background fabric, covering the top of the stem, and blind hem stitch around the edge. Iron the second three-petal shape on top, so all six petals can be seen, and blind hem stitch in place.

Making the Frayed Centre

7 Cut two 1¼in (3.2cm) squares of fabric for the centre of the flower. Using a pin or tweezers, remove threads from each side until you are left with a frayed square, with just under ½in (1.3cm) in the centre that's not frayed (Fig 2A).

8 Place the two squares on top of each other with the top one turned 45 degrees. With an easily removable marker, draw a circle about ⅜in (1cm) diameter in the centre of the square on top (Fig 2B). Hand sew a running stitch through both layers around the drawn circle. Leave the needle threaded, pull up the thread ends and knot securely. You should have something that looks like a shuttlecock (Fig 2C). Sew this piece to the centre of the clematis with the threaded needle.

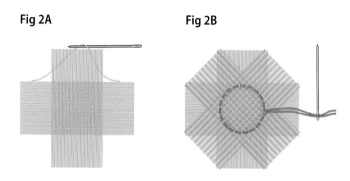

Fig 2A   **Fig 2B**

Fig 2C

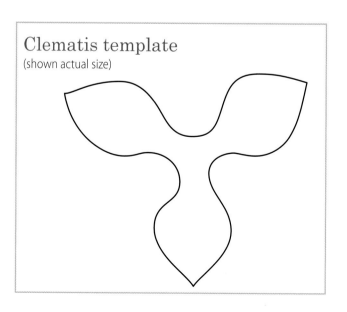

Clematis template
(shown actual size)

Design Inspirations...

Made by Geraldine Clarke

Made by Judith Jackman

Real clematis flowers grow in a wide variety of colours, especially modern cultivars, but of course you can use any shades for your fabric flowers, as these two examples show. The frayed centre is shown in pale colours but you could use variegated fabric for a more colourful look, or a colour to contrast with your fabrics. You could experiment further with petal colours by choosing a different colour or shade for each group of three petals.

I used four clematis flowers in my quilt block, alternating them with tulips, plus a plump chrysanthemum flower in the centre to hide the ends of the stems and give a focus to the design.

Cyclamen

The cyclamen is such a delicate flower and has an interesting twist to its petal formation, which can be re-created by layering the sewn petals. This was the last flower I designed for my quilt. Around Christmas time I had a lovely cyclamen in a pot on my windowsill, which kept saying, 'make one of me' – so here it is! The three-dimensional work is made easier by the use of fusible web.

REQUIREMENTS
- Background fabric, size according to your quilt block or project
- Fabric for stems, leaves, cyclamen and bud
- Machine sewing thread, cotton or polyester, to match fabrics
- Machine sewing thread, rayon, cotton or polyester, for satin stitching the leaves
- Small piece of tear-away stabilizer
- Wool for stuffing stems
- Small amount of wadding (batting) for leaves
- Fusible web
- Tube turner (optional)

Making the Stems

1 Cut one bias strip, 1⅛in x 4½in (2.9cm x 11.4cm) and one bias strip, 1in x 3½in (2.5cm x 8.9cm). Fold each strip in half lengthways, right sides together. Sew a ¼in (6mm) seam along the side of the smaller strip and along the side and one short end of the larger strip. Clip the seam allowances at the corner of the larger strip and turn both tubes through to the right side using a tube turner or needle and thread (see Turning Shapes to the Right Side in Techniques).

2 Stuff the large stem with two strands of thick wool and the smaller one with one strand. You can do this easily with a Fasturn gadget by placing the wool in the top of the tube before pulling it through. If you do not own this gadget then use the 'cradle' method, as follows. Fold a length of thread in half and thread the loop through the eye of a blunt needle (see Fig 1A). Bring the thread ends around the needle and knot them (Fig 1B). Thread a length of wool that is twice as long as the large stem through the loop of thread with the middle of the wool next to the loop (Fig 1C). Push the needle through the open end of the large stem, pulling the wool through with it. Bring the needle out through the top of the stem and cut off the thread that formed the cradle. For the narrow stem that has both ends open, simply thread the wool through a needle with a large eye and pull it through.

Fig 1A   **Fig 1B**

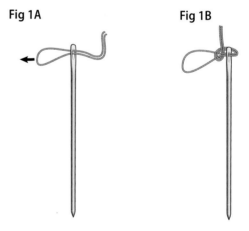

Fig 1C

Making the Petals

3 On the wrong side of the fabric, draw the petal 1 template five times, placing it so that the centre of the petal is on the bias grain. Leave about ½in (1.3cm) between each shape.

4 Place another piece of the same fabric underneath, so that right sides are facing. Sew around the edge of each petal but leave the bottom edge un-sewn. Trim about ⅛in (3mm) from the stitching lines.

5 Draw around the petal 2 template on a piece of fusible web five times and cut them out on the line. Iron a fusible web shape to one side of each petal. Peel off the backing paper and then turn each petal through to the right side. Iron them flat.

6 Layer five petals on top of each other as in Fig 2, with the left petal on top. It is very important that you layer the petals in this order otherwise it will cause problems when you sew them to the background. The ends that have the raw edges should measure about 1in (2.5cm) across.

> *Tip*
>
> Ideally, the petals should go around the stem with the first one overlapping the last one the same amount as the others are overlapping. However, depending upon the thickness of your fabric and the diameter of your stem, they may not be long enough to go around or may overlap too much. If this is the case, then adjust the width accordingly.

7 Place tear-away stabilizer underneath and sew across the ends of the petals, about ¼in (6mm) from the raw edges. Remove the stabilizer. Place the finished end of the thicker stem on top, with ⅛in (3mm) extending over the stitching and sew in place (Fig 3). Bring the ends of the petals together over the stem, overlapping the first and last petals to form a roll and hand sew in place (Fig 4).

8 Trim the raw edge to about two-thirds the original size. Flip the petals up and over the stem and hand sew in place, ¼in (6mm) from the end of the stem (Fig 5). Bring the stem down between two of the petals.

Fig 2

← 1in (2.5cm) →

Fig 3

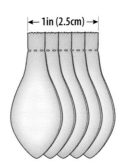

Fig 4

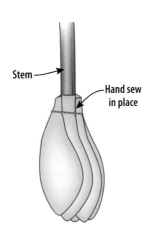

Stem

Hand sew in place

Fig 5

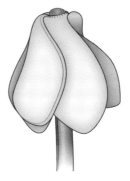

Positioning the Flower

9 Using an easily removable marker, copy the placement template on to your background fabric. Sew the petals to the background, shaping them as follows. Place the first petal on the background with the point in line with the top of the flower on your placement marks. The petal on the left should go under it, as in Fig 6. Secure with a small zigzag stitch at the right edge near the stem only so the tops of the petals are free.

10 Now sew the petal on the right of the one sewn, twisting it so that the right edge is flat against the background. Sew it to the background along the right-hand edge near the base only (Fig 7).

11 Place the next petal so the left-hand edge is in the middle of the first petal. Sew this one to the first petal along the middle of its left edge (Fig 8). Sew the middle of the left edge of the remaining petal so it is towards the left side of the first petal. The aim is to manipulate and sew the petals so the edges that are not sewn to the background will stand up. They don't have to look exactly like mine.

12 Trim away about 1in (2.5cm) of the wool from the other end of the stem and pin or glue it in position on the background. Blind hem stitch it in place, beginning at the end of the stem and stopping about 1in (2.5cm) away from the base of the flower.

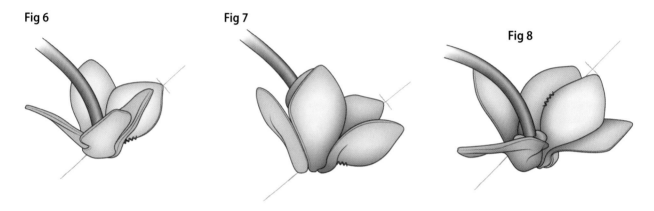

Fig 6   **Fig 7**   **Fig 8**

Making the Cyclamen Bud

13 On the wrong side of the fabric draw petal 3 template five times, placing it so that the centre of the petal is on the bias grain. Leave about ½in (1.3cm) between each shape.

14 Place another piece of the same fabric underneath, so that right sides are facing. Sew around the edge of each petal but leave the bottom edge un-sewn. Trim about ⅛in (3mm) from the stitching lines. Trim the point and turn each petal through to the right side.

15 To make a dart in the back of each petal, fold the fabric on the back in half lengthways, so the wrong sides are together and the seams are on top of each other. Draw a line from the raw edge at the top to the point at the bottom. It should be very tiny, about ¹⁄₁₆in (1.5mm) from the fold at the side and end ¼in (6mm) from the point at the bottom (Fig 9). Sew on the line.

16 Layer five petals on top of each other, with the darts underneath, so the top with the raw edges measures about ¾in–1in (2cm–2.5cm) across. Place tear-away stabilizer underneath and sew across the top of the petals, about ¼in (6mm) from the raw edges. Place the end of the thinner stem on top with ⅛in (3mm) extending over the stitching and sew in place (Fig 10).

Fig 9

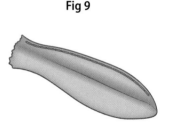

Fig 10

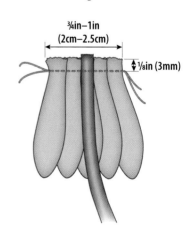

¾in–1in (2cm–2.5cm)

⅛in (3mm)

17 Join the first and last petals together over the stem, forming a roll and hand sew in place at the top (Fig 11). (See Tip under step 6 on sewing the cyclamen petals.) Bring the petals down, away from the stem, right side out. Sew the petals to each other, about ¼in (6mm) from the top, sewing the underside of the petal to the top of the next one so the stitching won't show on the front. Now sew the petals to each other at the tips, swirling them around slightly.

18 Pin the bud in place and trim away about 1in (2.5cm) of the wool from the other end of the stem. Pin or glue it in position (Fig 12). Blind hem stitch three-quarters of the stem to the background and then hand sew the bud in place.

Fig 11

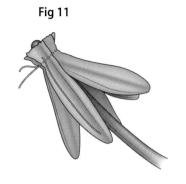

Fig 12

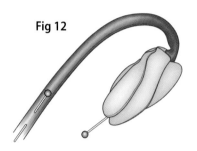

Making the Leaves

19 Draw three of the leaf templates on to the backing paper of the fusible web. Rough cut them out. Peel off the backing paper that isn't drawn on. Place the web side of the shapes on to the wrong side of your chosen leaf fabric. Fuse with an iron and then cut the leaves out on the lines. Peel off the second backing paper. Place a piece of wadding (batting) behind each leaf and then trim it about ¼in (6mm) from the edge of the leaf fabric.

20 Refer to the template for placement and iron leaf 1 in position at the ends of the stems. Satin stitch around the edge – see Satin Stitching in Techniques. Sew a triple stitch along the vein lines. Repeat for leaf 2 and then leaf 3 to finish.

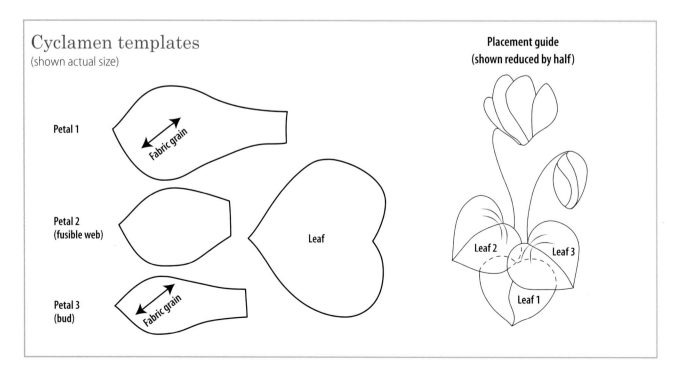

Cyclamen templates
(shown actual size)

Placement guide
(shown reduced by half)

Petal 1

Fabric grain

Petal 2
(fusible web)

Leaf

Petal 3
(bud)

Fabric grain

Leaf 2   Leaf 3

Leaf 1

Design Inspirations...

Made by Pauline Ineson

Made by Sandra Pirie

The cyclamen is such a delicate flower and the way its petals unfurl creates a lovely twist to the design. Colours used can be in the pink and purple range or why not be more adventurous and use graded fabric? Two examples are shown here to inspire you.

The cyclamen makes a lovely addition to a quilt block. The block in my quilt is a symmetrical design with a marigold in the centre. Four cyclamen flowers and their buds radiate out from this towards the corners, with clusters of berries added to fill in the design. The ends of the stems are hidden by cyclamen leaves. Crosshatch quilting completes the block.

Daffodil

The daffodil I've created here is very three dimensional and quite realistic and would look good in two shades – maybe a deep, almost orange centre and a paler yellow for the petals. Alternatively, you could go completely mad and use any colour you like, red, purple or even blue! The outer petals are double-sided shapes turned through to the right side, while the centre is formed by ruching and gathering a strip of fabric.

REQUIREMENTS
- Background fabric, size according to your quilt block or project
- Fabric for stem, 1in x 3in (2.5cm x 7.6cm) cut on the bias grain
- Fabric for leaves 3in (7.6cm) square
- Fabric for petals 5in x 8in (12.7cm x 20.3cm)
- Fabric for the centre 6in x 2½in (15.2cm x 6.3cm) cut on the bias
- Machine sewing thread to match fabrics
- Fusible web
- Embroidery cotton (floss) for the stamens, about 1yd (1m)
- Soft wool (yarn) to stuff the stem
- Easily removable fabric marker

Making the Stem

1 Cut one bias strip 1in x 3in (2.5cm x 7.6cm). Refer to Making Bias Stems in the General Techniques section to make the stem. Blind hem stitch the stem in place on your background fabric – refer to Blind Hem Stitching Appliqué. Stuff the stem with one strand of wool (yarn).

Making the Leaves

2 Using the templates at the end of the chapter, trace the two leaf shapes on to fusible web (I used Steam-A-Seam) and then cut them out on the line. Peel off the backing paper and iron the leaves to the wrong side of the leaf fabric, leaving about ½in (1.3cm) between each leaf for turnings.

3 Cut the fabric about ³⁄₁₆in (5mm) from the edge of the fusible web. Turn the edges over the web. Carefully remove the second backing paper and press the edges again. Appliqué the leaves on top of the daffodil stem, referring to the placement guide.

Making the Outer Petals

4 On the wrong side of the petal fabric and using the templates provided, draw around each of the six petals, leaving ½in (1.3cm) gap between them. Place another piece of the same fabric underneath, right sides together, and sew on the line, leaving a gap on the flat base of each petal. Trim the seam allowances and turn each petal through to the right side – refer to Turning Shapes Through to the Right Side.

5 Refer to the placement guide to pin petals 3 and 6 in position. Beginning at the base, sew a triple stitch down the centre of the petals, finishing about ½in (1.3cm) from the tip. Repeat this for petals 1 and 2 and again for petals 4 and 5. Trim any raw edges.

Making the Stamen

6 Take a single strand of embroidery cotton (floss) about 28in (71cm) long and fold it in half. Tie a single knot in the centre and cut the loop that is at one end (see Fig 1A).

7 Now twist the threads on your sewing machine's bobbin winder – see Making a Twisted Cord in the General Techniques section, making sure that you hold the knot when you bring the end to the bobbin. This will produce a little 'knob' at the folded end of the twisted cord (Fig 1B). Tie a knot in the other end to keep it twisted.

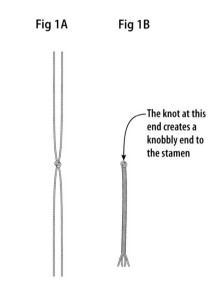

Fig 1A   **Fig 1B**

The knot at this end creates a knobbly end to the stamen

Making the Inner Petals

8 Cut a bias strip 6in x 2½in (15.2cm x 6.3cm) from your outer petal fabric. Fold it in half along the length, wrong sides together. On the right side, using an easily removable marker, draw a line ¼in (6mm) from the fold and another line ½in (1.3cm) from the fold. Place a mark every ½in (1.3cm) along the top line, beginning and ending at the raw edges on the sides. Begin ¾in (2cm) from the raw edge at the side of the second line and mark every ½in (1.3cm), finishing ¾in (2cm) from the raw edge at the other end (Fig 2). Now join the marks, forming a zigzag line for ruching.

Fig 2

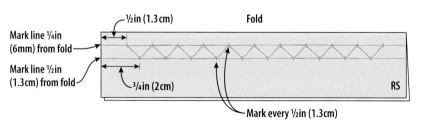

½in (1.3cm)   Fold

Mark line ¼in (6mm) from fold

Mark line ½in (1.3cm) from fold

¾in (2cm)

Mark every ½in (1.3cm)

RS

9 Turn the fabric piece over and draw a line on the other side a scant ¼in (6mm) from the raw edge along the bottom. Open out the strip, bring the short ends together right sides facing and sew a ½in (1.3cm) seam (Fig 3A). Trim the seam allowances to between ⅛in–¼in (3mm–6mm) above the fold line and slightly less below the fold line (Fig 3B). Press the seam open.

Fig 3A

Fig 3B

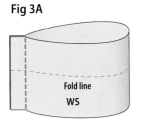
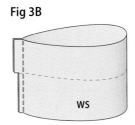

10 Fold the strip in half again, wrong sides together as before and turn the tube so that the ruching marks you made earlier are facing inside the tube (Fig 4). Beginning at a point that isn't over the seam, machine sew along the zigzag line, length 3.5, tension loosened slightly. Do not secure the stitches at the beginning and end and leave thread tails. You may find it easier to use a narrow foot to navigate the small gap. Make sure you sew all the way around the tube so the last stitch meets the first one.

Fig 4

11 Turn the tube inside out so that the ¼in (6mm) line above the raw edge at the bottom is on the inside. Machine a gathering stitch along this line. Pull up the bobbin thread tails of the line at the bottom as tightly as possible, knot them securely and bury them. Stretch the folded edge a little before pulling up the ruching thread tails. Knot the ends and bury them.

 *Tip* When pulling up thread tails, the bobbin thread is usually the easiest one to pull. You can tie off, cut and bury the top threads first to get them out of the way but be careful not to pull the threads otherwise they will lock the stitches and prevent you from pulling up the bobbin threads.

12 Flip the outer part of the daffodil so the inside is on the outside and the gathers at the bottom are inside the flower (Fig 5). Push the tip of a stamen through the centre of the flower from the back until it is the desired length. Knot and sew this to the back of the flower to prevent it from pulling through. Trim the tails of the stamen and then securely hand sew the flower to the centre of the outer petals.

Fig 5

Raw edges of gathered fabric

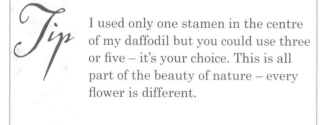

Tip

I used only one stamen in the centre of my daffodil but you could use three or five – it's your choice. This is all part of the beauty of nature – every flower is different.

Daffodil templates
(shown actual size)

Placement guide

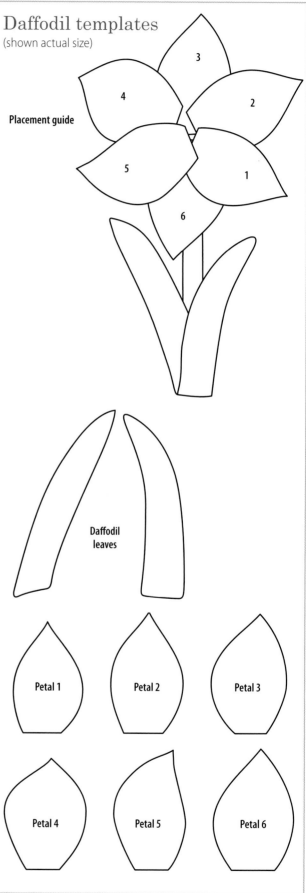

Daffodil leaves

Petal 1

Petal 2

Petal 3

Petal 4

Petal 5

Petal 6

Design Inspirations...

Made by Sandra Pirie

Made by Sallie Hopper

Daffodils are perennial favourites in gardening and embroidery and these pretty flowers have a lovely three-dimensional quality and are well worth the effort. Colourwise, anything goes, from a pure deep yellow all over, to bi-coloured petals or more unusual colours and fabric prints.

I have teamed the daffodils in my quilt block with pink carnations and a beautiful gazania in the centre, made using a Cathedral Window technique.

This block forms the centre of the quilt and is given more emphasis by Dresden Plate appliqué behind the flowers.

Foxglove

The statuesque foxglove makes a wonderful subject for three-dimensional stitching. The flower looks best when the inside and outside fabrics contrast with each other. I'm lucky because I see all the different colour choices my ladies have made – see some examples at the end of this chapter. A mottled or dotty fabric works well for the inside of the flowers. The distinctive tubular shape and a satin stitch edging really bring this flower to life.

REQUIREMENTS

- Background fabric, size according to your quilt block or project
- Fabric for the stem, outsides, insides and tops of foxgloves
- Machine sewing thread in cotton or polyester to match fabrics
- Rayon, polyester or cotton thread for satin stitching edges
- Fusible web
- Water-soluble stabilizer
- Cord or wool to stuff the stem
- Embroidery hoop (optional)

Making the Stem

1 Cut one bias strip, 1⅛in x 4in (2.9cm x 10.2cm) and make the stem – see Making Bias Stems in the Techniques section.

2 Use a fabric glue stick or pins to secure the stem to your background and then sew it using a blind hem stitch or similar – see Blind Hem Stitching Appliqué. Now stuff the stem using wool or cord.

Making the Flower

3 On a piece of fusible web (the side with the web attached) and using the templates at the end of this chapter, draw around each foxglove shape twice (petals 1, 2, 3), making sure they are all facing in the same direction. Roughly cut around the outside of each drawing.

4 Remove the backing paper that hasn't been drawn on and place the drawn shapes, web side down on the wrong side of the outer foxglove fabric so the lower, wavy edges, of the petals are on the bias grain. Press with an iron and cut the petals out on the lines. Peel off the backing paper.

5 Iron these shapes to the inner fabric of the foxglove (but not at the point), wrong sides together, placing the lower edges on the bias grain.

6 Cut the inner fabric around the edges of the petals using the outer fabric as a guide. At the top point of each petal, peel the inner fabric back and trim it about ⅝in (1.6cm) from the point.

7 Sandwich a petal, inner fabric on top, between two layers of water-soluble stabilizer. Thread your machine with the same thread top and bottom to match or blend with the fabric. I used a 40 weight rayon. Select a satin stitch, width 2.5, and adjust the tension so the stitch looks the same on both sides. You may have to tighten the tension slightly (a higher number) if your machine sets the stitch automatically. Satin stitch around the lower edge of the petals so the needle swings just over the edge and then on to the fabric (see Fig 1). You may find it easier to hoop the stabilizer sandwich and use a metal or Teflon foot rather than a plastic one. You can use tear-away stabilizer instead but this can leave a white edge where it has been torn away. You may even be able to sew the edge without a stabilizer, so experiment first.

Fig 1

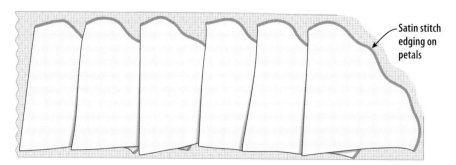

Satin stitch edging on petals

8 To avoid wasting the stabilizer, sew the first petal and then tear off the top layer of stabilizer. Overlap the next petal, replace the stabilizer and sew the edge. Repeat for the remaining petals. Tear off the stabilizer. Fold the top point over ½in (1.3cm) towards the inner fabric.

9 Bring wrong sides together (with inner fabric touching) and pin just above the satin stitching so the bottom edges are even. Sew a narrow seam, about ⅛in (3mm) (Fig 2). To prevent thread ends from showing along the bottom edge, start ½in (1.3cm) above the lower edge and sew to the end. Leave the needle down, turn the fabric 180 degrees, sew to the top and fix the ends. Iron seams open.

Fig 2

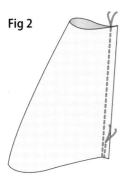

10 Join the petals together in pairs of the same size, dropping the ones on the right down about ¼in (6mm) so the bottom edges are uneven (Fig 3). Use a bridging stitch, L:1.5, W:1.5 or 2.0 (see Fig 4), a zigzag stitch or sew by hand. The seam should be at the back, closer to the centre of the two petals than the outside edge.

Fig 3

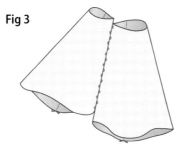

Fig 4

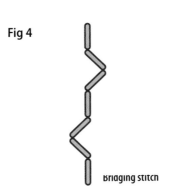

Bridging stitch

11 Place the pair of large petals over the stem so the tops are 3in (7.6cm) from the end of the stem. Pin through the centre of the petal pair to the background. Sew a straight stitch down the centre of the pair to secure to the background. Peel back the side of one petal so that the seam allowance is just under the folded edge. Move the flower slightly towards the centre to eliminate any gap between the two. Blind stitch in place (Fig 5). Sew the side of the other petal in the same way

Fig 5

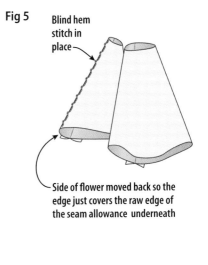

Blind hem stitch in place

Side of flower moved back so the edge just covers the raw edge of the seam allowance underneath

12 Repeat this procedure for the medium-sized petal pair, placing the tops 4in (10.2cm) from the end of the stem. Repeat for the small petal pair, placing the tops 5in (12.7cm) from the end.

Making the Calyx

13 Place two pieces of fabric, about 1in (2.5cm) square, right sides together. On the wrong side of the fabric, draw around the shape (see Copying a Template).

14 With a straight stitch, length 1.5, sew around the shape on the lines. Cut around the outside of the stitching, leaving a seam allowance of about ⅛in (3mm). Make a small slit in the back and turn the shape through to the right side and press flat with an iron (see Turning Shapes to the Right Side).

15 Sew the calyx to the top of the foxglove using either a buttonhole appliqué stitch or blind hem stitch along the top and sides only.

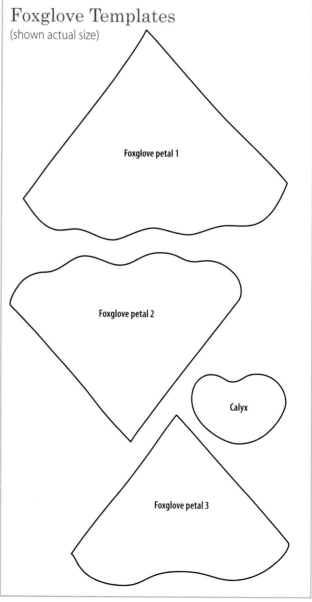

Foxglove Templates
(shown actual size)

Foxglove petal 1

Foxglove petal 2

Calyx

Foxglove petal 3

Design Inspirations...

Made by Katie George

Made by Sandra Pirie

The foxglove flowers can be made in many different prints and colour combinations, from traditional delicate floral prints and spots to more funky modern interpretations. Some examples are shown here to give you inspiration.

The foxglove block in my quilt is another symmetrical one. In each foxglove the three pairs of flowers graduate from large to small towards the corners of the block. A gerbera flower was sewn to the centre. As well as crosshatching the background, I also quilted in the ditch and around the appliqué on each of the flower squares.

Fuchsia

Fuchsias are beautifully coloured and so dainty with their stamens peeping through the centre. I think they look best if you use two contrasting fabrics – one for the inner petals and one for the outer ones. Pinks or purples are the most popular colour choices but you could go for a totally different, more contemporary look and use blues or oranges. The flower looks complicated but is really very simple to construct.

REQUIREMENTS
- Background fabric, size according to your quilt block or project
- Fabric for the stem, the inside and the outside of the fuchsia
- Machine sewing thread in cotton or polyester to match fabrics
- Decorative cord for the fuchsia stamens
- Seam sealant liquid

Making the Inner Petals

1 To make the centres, draw around the inner petal template four times on the wrong side of the fabric, leaving about ½in (1.3cm) between each one.

2 Place another piece of the same fabric right sides together and sew on the line, leaving a gap where indicated (see Copying a Template in Techniques). Trim both layers about ⅛in (3mm) from the seam line and turn the petals through to the right side (see Turning Shapes to the Right Side).

3 Lay four petals on top of each other and fan them out so that the bottom edges are about ¼in (6mm) apart and the top edges are about ⅛in (3mm) apart (see Fig 1). Machine a straight stitch along the top edges to hold them in place.

Fig 1

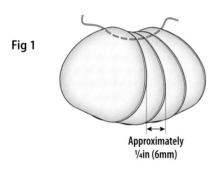

Approximately
¼in (6mm)

4 Bring the first petal round so the edge lies beneath the last petal, forming a tight roll at the top. Hand sew the tops of the first and last petals together. Continue with the same thread to secure each petal to the one next to it, about ¼in (6mm) from the raw edges at the top (Fig 2).

Fig 2

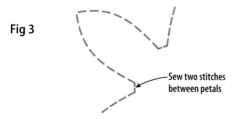

Secure with
hand stitches

Making the Outer Petals

5 For the outer petals, draw around the outer petal template on the wrong side of the fabric. Place another piece of the same fabric underneath, right sides together. Sew a straight stitch, length 2.0, on the line, sewing two stitches between each of the petals at the centre (Fig 3).

Fig 3

Sew two stitches
between petals

6 Cut the fabric ⅛in–¼in (3mm–6mm) from the stitching line. Apply a drop of seam sealant such as Fray Check at the points and between the petals at the centre. When dry, clip the seam allowances where they have the sealant. Cut a slit in the centre of the fabric at the back. Turn the petals through to the right side and press with an iron.

7 In the centre, on the front (the outside) of the five-petal shape, draw a 1in (2.5cm) diameter circle, or around a suitable coin using a removable fabric marker. In the centre, on the back (the inside) draw a ¼in (6mm) circle. Thread a hand sewing needle with a matching colour and bring the ends together so the thread is double. Sew the gap closed.

8 Using the same thread, sew the petals you made earlier to the ¼in (6mm) circle, sewing the sides at the top of each centre petal to a quarter of the circle. Secure the threads and bury the ends.

9 On the front, sew a small gathering stitch around the 1in (2.5cm) circle and then pull the ends to gather it, so that it surrounds the tops of the centre petals. Sew the outer petals to the inner ones at the centre where necessary to make sure the raw edges are hidden.

Making the Stamens

10 To make the stamens, for each fuchsia cut six 8in (20.3cm) lengths of embroidery thread. Tie a double knot at one end of each. Trim the thread close to the knot and apply a drop of seam sealant to prevent it from undoing.

11 Thread the knotted strands through a needle and bring the needle up through the inside of the fuchsia and out through the top. Adjust the stamens to the desired length and then tie them together on the inside, next to the top (you will have to pull them out of the flower to do this).

12 Place the lower end of the fuchsia under a heavy object to keep it still. Divide the stamen ends that are extending from the top of the fuchsia into three groups of two and then plait them together. Knot the ends.

Making the Stem

13 Cut a 1in x 6in (2.5cm x 15.2cm) bias strip. Turn a ¼in (6mm) hem, wrong sides together, at one short end (Fig. 4). Make this into a stem – see Making Bias Stems in Techniques.

Fig 4

Turn ¼in (6mm) to the wrong side

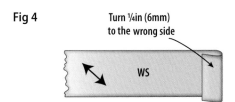

WS

14 Using a large-eyed needle, thread the stamen cords at the top of the fuchsia through the finished end of the stem and out through the top. Blind hem stitch the stem in place and sew the top of the fuchsia to the end of the stem. Hand sew the backs of two of the outer petals to the background to keep them in place.

Fuchsia templates
(shown actual size)

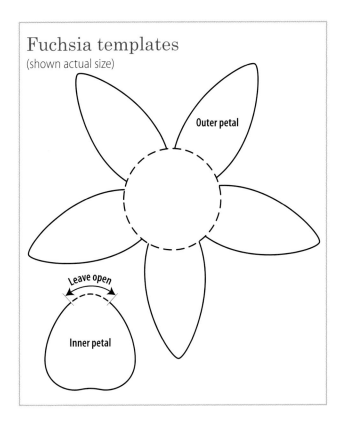

Outer petal

Leave open

Inner petal

Design Inspirations...

Made by Sallie Hopper

Made by Sandra Pirie

Fuchsias are commonly coloured pink, white, red, lilac and purple but you can change the colour to suit you and your project. In fact, you can go quite dotty as these examples show.

For the block in my quilt I designed the flowers to hang from the stems and added some berries for a contrasting shape. The fuchsia that overhangs one of the stems was originally a bud but I changed it after my daughter said it looked like a pink caterpillar!

Gerbera

This large, ruched flower is an ideal bloom to put in the centre of a block as it needs no stem. I sewed a tiny covered button in the middle but you can leave it without or choose a pretty button or bead instead – it also helps to hide any imperfections and I'm all for that! The ruching technique is easy to do and begins with a long strip of fabric.

REQUIREMENTS
- Background fabric, size according to your quilt block or project
- Main fabric 2¼in x 15½in (5.7cm x 39.4cm) strip, cut on the bias grain
- Polyester machine sewing thread 50 weight to match your fabric
- Easily removable fabric marker
- Small button or bead for the centre (optional)

Making the Flower

1 Cut a bias strip 2¼in x 15½in (5.7cm x 39.4cm). On the wrong side draw a line 1in (2.5cm) from one of the long edges. Fold the raw edge to the line, wrong sides together, giving a ½in (1.3cm) hem. Along the folded edge, mark every 1in (2.5cm), beginning and ending ¼in (6mm) from the raw edges of the short sides. Mark along the raw edge above the fold every 1in (2.5cm), beginning and ending ¾in (2cm) from the short sides (Fig 1). Using a fade-away marker, draw a line to connect the marks, forming a zigzag line.

Fig 1

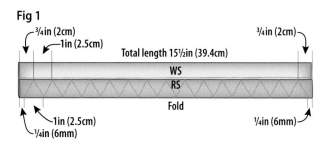

2 Open out the folded edge at the ends and join the short ends, right sides together, with a ¼in (6mm) seam (Fig 2). Press the seam open and fold up the edge again.

Fig 2

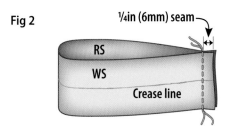

3 Sew a machine gathering stitch, L: 3.5, tension slightly looser, along the zigzag line beginning at a point on the raw edge that has been folded up and about 1in (2.5cm) from the seam (Fig 3). Do not fix or secure the stitching at either end. Leave long thread tails for pulling up later. Bobbin thread should match the fabric as this stitching will show on the front. Make sure you sew all the way around the tube, ending at the point where you started. When you sew the stitching for the ruching, choose a thread that is less likely to break – 50 weight polyester thread is stronger than 60 weight (bobbin thread) and cotton or rayon thread.

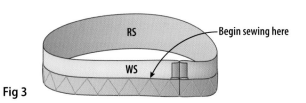

Fig 3

4 Divide the circle into eighths by folding in half, in half again and in half again, placing a pin or mark at each fold. Bring the right sides together at the first mark and sew a dart ½in (1.3cm) in from the fold at the top raw edge and sew down and off the edge to about ¼in (6mm) above the raw edge that has been folded up (Fig 4). Repeat for the other marks. Trim, and iron the darts open.

Fig 4

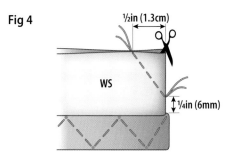

5 With the wrong side up, sew a line of gathering stitches between the two raw edges (Fig 5). Again, your bobbin thread needs to match your fabric.

Fig 5

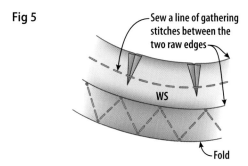

6 Pull up the zigzag gathering threads that are on the right side (the bobbin thread) to form the petals until the piece measures about 3¼in (8.25cm) across the middle when folded in half (Fig 6). Tie off and bury the thread ends.

Fig 6

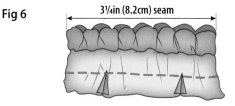

7 On the wrong side hand sew a gathering stitch about ¼in (6mm) from the top raw edge. Use double thread and a short stitch on top and long stitch underneath. Pull up the thread ends as tightly as possible and knot them. If the centre doesn't pull up closed, then sew across the gathering a few times, pulling the thread tightly. Knot the thread ends again and bury them.

8 Turn the flower to the right side so that the centre is turned inwards to the back. (Alternatively, bring the gathered raw edge to the front and have a flower with a frayed centre.) Pull up the remaining row of gathering stitches in the area between the centre and the edge from the right side until the flower lays flat. Sew the button or bead in position, if using. Tie off and bury all loose ends.

Making a Different Size Flower

It is easy to vary the size of the flower, bearing the following points in mind.
Width of bias strip = half the finished flower diameter, from the outside edges of the petals, plus ¾in (2cm). For a 4in (10.2cm) diameter flower you will need to cut the strips 3¼in (8.25cm) wide. Length of the bias strip = the number of petal in inches plus ½in (1.3cm). For a seventeen-petal flower you will need to cut the strips 17½in (44.4cm) long.

Design Inspirations...

Made by Sandra Pirie

Made by Katie George

A large flower such as the gerbera is very useful as a three-dimensional focal point in a design or as a single decoration, which can be used rather like a fabric yoyo. The examples here show that the colours and fabrics really can be anything you choose – plain or patterned, subtle or bright.

For the block in my quilt I placed the gerbera in the centre of the foxgloves as it covered the stems nicely and was a good contrasting shape. I sewed a tiny covered button in the centre. For this button I 'fussy cut' the fabric, so I had a little flower motif showing on the top.

Lily

The lily is such a gorgeous flower and so deserving of a place in a floral quilt. There are different lily shapes, including trumpet and oriental. Mine is based on an Asiatic type and I've made it in a dusky pink, although almost any colour would look good. The lily I've created is very simple to make, using six petal shapes, which are blind hem stitched into place. A cluster of stamens is made from twisted cord and each stamen is finished with a tiny seed bead.

REQUIREMENTS

- Background fabric, size according to your quilt block or project
- Fabric for petals about 9in x 3in (23cm x 7.6cm)
- Machine sewing thread to match fabric
- Fusible web
- Wadding (batting) about 9in x 3in (23cm x 7.6cm)
- Embroidery cotton (floss) or similar for the stamens
- Five small beads for the stamen ends

Making the Petals

1 Using the templates at the end of the chapter, trace the petal shapes for the lily on to fusible web (I used Steam-A-Seam) and then cut them out on the line. Peel off the backing paper and iron the shapes to the wrong side of the fabric, placing them on the bias grain where possible and leaving about 1in (2.5cm) between each for turnings.

2 Cut the fabric about ³⁄₁₆in (5mm) from the edge of the fusible web. Turn the edges over the web (see Turning Raw Edges to the Wrong Side in the General Techniques section. Do not turn the edge along the dashed lines. Remove the second backing paper (if using Steam-A-Seam) and then press the edges again.

3 Place a piece of wadding (batting) under each petal and tack (baste) in place. Trim the wadding just under the edges of the petals so that it doesn't show from the front. Blind hem stitch petals 1 to 5 in order on your background fabric (see Blind Hem Stitching Appliqué). Remove the tacking (basting) stitches.

Fig 1

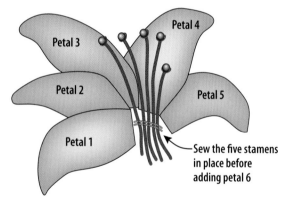

Sew the five stamens in place before adding petal 6

4 Referring to Making a Twisted Cord in Techniques, make the five stamens with a bead at the end of each. Sew these in place under where the last petal will go, using a triple stitch (Fig 1). Trim the ends. Blind hem stitch petal 6 in place and remove the tacking stitches. To finish, sew a triple stitch down the centre of each petal to represent the vein. See the chapter on Leaves for ideas on leaves to accompany this flower.

Lily templates
(shown actual size)

Petal 2

Petal 3

Petal 4

Petal 1

Petal 5

Petal 6

Design Inspirations...

Made by Sandra Pirie

Made by Sallie Hopper

Lilies grow in a wonderful variety of colours, particularly since modern hybridization – from pure white to the darkest maroon, and including all shades of pink, red, orange and yellow. Many lilies have gorgeous spots and blotches on their petals and careful choice of fabrics could show these effects. The variations here show how the flower is enhanced by the addition of little beads on the ends of the stamens.

The lily flower has been used in my quilt with pansies and bell flowers, balancing the leaf cluster at the base of the block. This cluster of leaves is a useful motif and is described in the Leaves chapter.

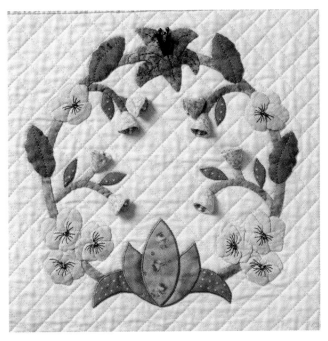

Lily of the Valley

These dainty lily of the valley flowers are a little fiddly to make but I think they are well worth the effort, especially when you see the finished result arching so prettily along its stem. They suit delicate shades and look utterly charming with a little pearl bead peeping out of the flower hood. The flowers start with a simple rectangle of fabric, which is folded and sewn with a picot stitch to create the distinctive fluted edge.

REQUIREMENTS

- Background fabric, size according to your quilt block or project
- Fabric for six little flowers cut on bias 2½in x 9in (6.3cm x 23cm)
- Fabric for stem 1in x 6in (2.5cm x 15.2cm) cut on bias (optional)
- Machine sewing thread to match fabric
- Easily removable fabric marker
- Seam sealant liquid
- Small amount of toy stuffing
- One bead 4mm diameter for each flower

Making the Stem

1 The individual lily of the valley flowers can be sewn directly on to the background fabric or be placed along a curving stem. If you want to include a stem, use a strip of fabric cut on the bias and refer to Making Bias Stems in the General Techniques section.

Making an Individual Flower

2 Cut a rectangle of fabric on the bias grain, 2½in x 1½in (6.3cm x 3.8cm). Using an easily removable marker, draw a line on the wrong side 1¼in (3.2cm) above one of the longer raw edges and then fold the edge to the line. Iron the fold flat.

3 With the right side up, sew a picot stitch along the folded edge (Fig 1). You will need to shorten the stitch length so that the zigzags are a little over ¼in (6mm) apart and tighten the tension to the highest number. Line up the fabric under the foot with the folded edge on the right-hand side, making sure that the right swing of the needle sews just over the folded edge and the left swing goes into the fabric (Fig 2). Because the tension has been tightened and the fabric is on the bias grain, it will pull up at each zigzag stitch, forming a fluted edge. If your machine doesn't have this stitch, you might be able to adjust the blind hem stitch by either mirror imaging it or positioning the fabric so the fold is on the left. If you don't have a blind hem stitch either, then draw a small zigzag line for ruching (similar to that used on Fig 2 of the Daffodil), sew a gathering stitch along the line and pull up the threads after the seams have been sewn (later in step 6).

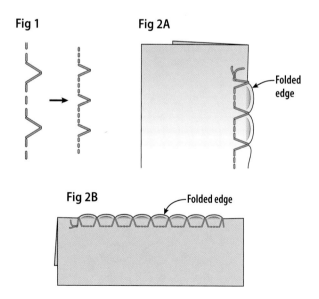

Fig 1

Fig 2A

Folded edge

Fig 2B

Folded edge

4 Now bring the wrong sides together so the first and last 'dips' on the edge are on top of themselves (Fig 3). Sew a seam about ⅜in (1cm) long from the folded edge. To prevent thread tails at the edge, begin ⅜in (1cm) from the edge, and sew towards it.

When you reach the edge, leave the needle in the fabric, pivot 180 degrees and sew a few stitches back up the seam (Fig 4).

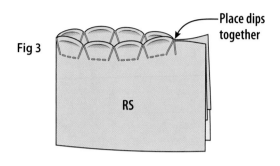

Fig 3

Place dips together

RS

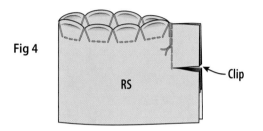

Fig 4

RS

Clip

5 Clip the seam allowance at the end of the stitching. Turn the shape through so the wrong side is on the outside. Bring the raw edges that are above the seam to the outside and sew them together (Fig 5). Flatten the tube so the seam is at the back in the middle. Using an easily removable marker, draw an arc from side to side with the top about ⅛in (3mm) from the raw edges at the top and curving down to the top of the raw edge that was folded up in step 1 (see Fig 6).

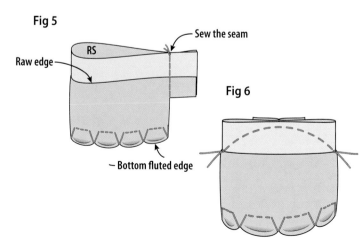

Fig 5

RS

Raw edge

Sew the seam

Fig 6

Bottom fluted edge

6 Sew a gathering stitch along the line (stitch length 3.0, do not secure the stitches at the beginning or end and loosen the tension slightly, i.e., a lower number). Pull up the bobbin thread to gather the top, knot the ends and trim them. Trim off the corners. Turn the shape through to the right side. Apply a drop of seam sealant such as Fray Check at the bottom seam and when dry, trim the seam allowance that is on the outside at the back quite close to the stitching so it doesn't show from the front (Fig 7).

7 Beginning at the seam, hand sew a gathering stitch about ¼in (6mm) above the fluting along the lower edge. Pull the thread up tightly to gather it. Leave the thread tails to sew the flower to the background. Using a tiny amount of stuffing, lightly stuff the top part of the flower above the gathering.

Making the Stamen

8 Make a stamen with bead attached by referring to Making a Twisted Cord. Thread the end of the stamen through the opening at the bottom of the lily and out through the top, catching the stuffing in the process.

9 You will need to make about six individual flowers for each lily of the valley spray. When all the flowers are made, sew them into position on the background fabric. If you have made a stem then sew the flowers in place along the stem. Using a needle with a large eye, pull the stamen end through the background until the stamen is the correct length – the bead should show just under the gathering stitches. Knot the ends at the back. Hand sew the back of the flower to the background, hiding the seam at the bottom in the process. See the Leaves chapter for ideas on leaves to accompany this flower.

Fig 7

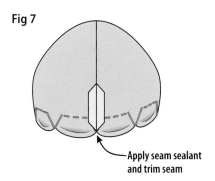

Apply seam sealant
and trim seam

Made by Pauline Ineson

Design Inspirations...

Lilies of the valley are such delicate flowers and once the individual florets have been made and arranged in a gentle arch they look so pretty. The examples shown here use pale shades but you could experiment with bolder colours for a different look. The glistening bead in the centre of each flower is a lovely finishing touch.

The lily of the valley spray in my quilt block is arranged with bunches of grapes and leaves curving around an intertwining circular design.

Marigold

The marigold is a joyful little flower in all its bright summery colours. It also looks very pretty in multi-print fabric. This is another flower that would be good to use for the centre of a design as it doesn't need a stem. The ruffled centre is easy to make and offers an opportunity to add a second colour to the flower. The technique for creating the flower is quite simple, using ruching, gathering and then coiling the fabric.

REQUIREMENTS

- Background fabric, size according to your quilt block or project
- Fabric for flower 1¾in x 20in (4.4cm x 51cm) bias strip
- Fabric for flower centre two 1¼in (3.2cm) squares (optional)
- Wadding (batting) about 3in (7.6cm) square (optional)
- Machine sewing thread to match fabrics
- A wide bias bar
- An easily removable marker
- Tear-away stabilizer
- Fusible web for leaves

Making the Flower

1 Cut a bias strip 1¾in x 20in (4.4cm x 51cm). Fold the strip in half, wrong sides together, along the length and sew a ¼in seam (6mm). Place the strip on a wide bias bar and iron the seam open. Remove the bias bar and press again, making sure the seam is in the centre. Trim the seam allowances to half their original width.

2 To mark the gathering line, place the strip front side up (the side without the seam) and use a removable marker. Begin at the raw edge at one end and place a dot every 1¼in (3.2cm) along the folded edge at the top. To mark the fold at the bottom of the strip, begin ⅝in (1.6cm) in from the raw edge at the end and mark every 1¼in (3.2cm) (Fig 1). Join the dots to form a zigzag line.

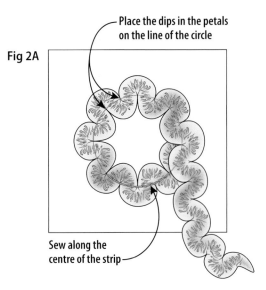

Fig 2A

Place the dips in the petals on the line of the circle

Sew along the centre of the strip

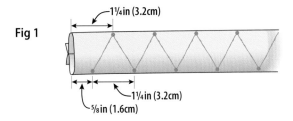

Fig 1

1¼in (3.2cm)

1¼in (3.2cm)

⅝in (1.6cm)

3 Machine along the zigzag line with a straight stitch, length 3.5. Do not secure the stitches at the beginning and end but leave thread tails and loosen the tension a little (lower number). Select the needle down position if you have one to make it easier to pivot at the points of the zigzag line. Pull up the bobbin thread so the strip measures about 9in (23cm). Knot the thread ends and even out the gathers.

4 Place two squares of tear-away stabilizer (about 3in/7.6cm square) on top of each other and draw a 1½in (3.8cm) diameter circle in the centre of the top square. Bring the start of the ruffle just inside the circle and then pin the ruffle to the stabilizer so the dips in the petals are on the drawn circle (Fig 2A). Stop when you have pinned all the way around the outside of the circle (you will be left with some of the ruffle not yet pinned to the stabilizer) and then sew down the centre of the ruffle, stitch length 4.0 (Fig 2B).

5 Continue pinning the ruffle in decreasing circles on the inside of the ruffle you have sewn to the stabilizer, with the pinheads facing outwards. Tuck the end of the ruffle under at the centre so the raw edges are hidden. If needed, trim off the ends of the ruffle close to the first and last gathering stitches. Machine down the centre of the ruffle, peeling back any of the ruffle that is lying on top and in the way. Tear off the stabilizer that is showing around the outside of the flower.

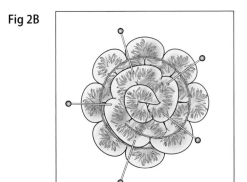

Fig 2B

Making the Frayed Centre

6 This part is optional. Cut two 1¼in (3.2cm) squares from your chosen fabric. Using a pin or tweezers, remove threads from each side until you are left with a frayed square, with just under ½in (1.3cm) in the centre that's not frayed (Fig 3A).

7 Place the two squares on top of each other with the top one turned 45 degrees. With an easily removable marker, draw a circle about ⅜in (1cm) diameter in the centre of the square on top (Fig 3B). Hand sew a running stitch through both layers around the drawn circle. Leave the needle threaded, pull up the thread ends and knot securely. You should have something that looks like a shuttlecock (Fig 3C). Finish by sewing this piece to the centre of the flower with the threaded needle.

Fig 3A   **Fig 3B**   **Fig 3C**

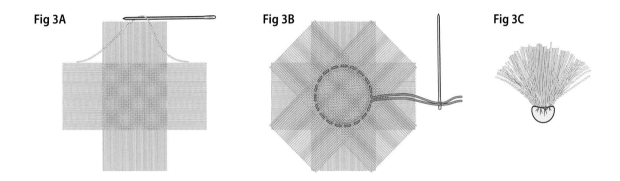

Design Inspirations...

Made by Julie Whitehouse

Made by Sallie Hopper

Marigold flowers are very useful as they can be made in any size and any colour, so can be used as a focal point or to scatter around other flowers. The examples here show how different they can look when made in a bold patterned fabric compared to a plainer colour.

I have used the marigold in two of the blocks for my quilt. In both blocks the flower is placed at the centre of the block as a focal point. Added stems and leaves bring a nice symmetry to the design.

Pansy

What a cheerful little flower the pansy is, and so distinctive with the dark central markings on its petals. The flower can be created in fabric using a wide range of colours, from pale cream to the deepest purple. You can also fussy cut the fabric if desired, to mimic the splotches of contrasting colour at the base of each petal. These areas are accented with some machine stitching and the addition of a few tiny seed beads.

REQUIREMENTS

- Background fabric, size according to your quilt block or project
- Fabric, for the petals about 8in x 3in (20.3cm x 7.6cm)
- Machine sewing thread to match fabric
- Contrasting thread for the accent lines
- Point turner or similar
- Two or three small beads

Making the Petals

1 I have given two different pansy designs, labelled A and B. Both of these could be reversed (AR and BR) to give two more designs. Each pansy has five petals but only four templates are needed, as template 2 forms two of the petals. Choose a design and use the relevant templates. Draw around each petal on to the wrong side of the fabric (refer to Copying a Template). Place each shape on the fabric bias where possible and leave ¾in (2cm) between them to allow for turnings. Place the fabric, drawn side up, on to the right side of another piece of the same fabric. Sew a straight stitch on the line, length 1.5, leaving a gap where a dotted line is marked on petals 2, 3 and 4 (for turning shapes to the right side).

2 Trim the fabric ⅛in (3mm) from the sewing line and clip all curves and points. Turn each petal to the right side through the gap on petals 2, 3 and 4 (refer to Turning Shapes to the Right Side). Make a small slit in the centre of the fabric on the back of petal 1 (the fabric not drawn on). Use a point turner or similar on the inside of the seam to define the edges. Iron each petal flat.

3 Layer the petals to form the pansy following the placement guide and mark the accent lines on petals 1 and 2. Remove the petals and using a contrasting thread and a straight stitch, machine sew the accent lines (Fig 1). Begin sewing at the base and then to the top of the first accent line. Pivot at the top and sew back towards the base, on top of the first line of stitching. Repeat for each accent line.

Fig 1

Start here ·
Pivot

4 Pin petal 4 to the background and sew a small zigzag stitch at the base to secure it. Repeat for petal 3. Blind hem stitch petal 2 and petal 1 in place. Hand sew two or three small beads in the centre of each pansy. See the Leaves chapter for ideas on leaves.

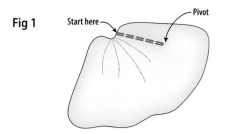

Placement guide for Shape A flower petals

Shape A

Shape AR

Placement guide for Shape B flower petals

Shape B

Shape BR

Pansy templates

(shown actual size)

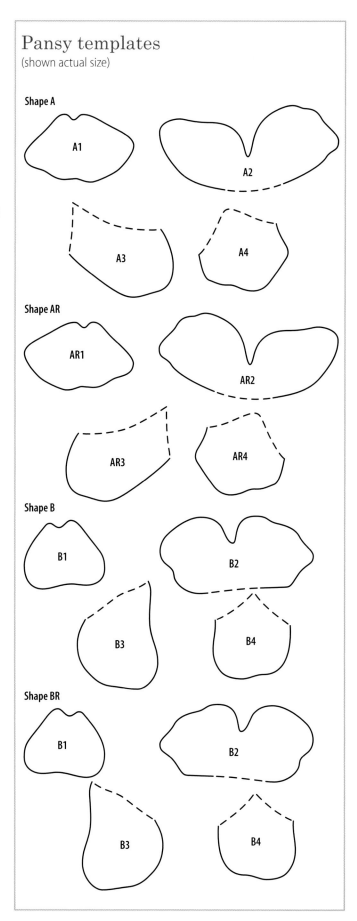

Shape A

A1

A2

A3

A4

Shape AR

AR1

AR2

AR3

AR4

Shape B

B1

B2

B3

B4

Shape BR

B1

B2

B3

B4

Design Inspirations...

Made by Sallie Hopper

Made by Katherine Willis

Creating three-dimensional pansies is great fun and the accent stitching makes all the difference. I chose a creamy yellow for my flowers as this colour suited my quilt design but almost any colour works, as these two examples show. A marbled pink is very pretty, while the purple version looks very realistic with the pink splotches on the fabric.

For my quilt block I combined single pansies and triple groupings with some little bell flowers and a single pink lily. The leaf cluster at the base of the block anchors the design and this is described in the Leaves chapter.

Passion Flower

The passion flower or passiflora has an intriguing structure of petals and thin filaments surrounding the central anthers. My fabric version isn't meant to be realistic and is really three flowers in one. The outer flower has eight pointed petals, created with reverse appliqué. Within this is a flower with six rounded petals, and then a ruched flower with a frayed centre. This flower is ideal to use as a centre design in a quilt block as it doesn't need a stem.

REQUIREMENTS
- Background fabric, size according to your quilt block or project
- Fabric for the reverse appliqué 'window' 4in (10.2cm) square
- Fabric for the six-petal flower two 4in (10.2cm) squares
- Fabric for the ruched flower 1¼in (3.2cm) wide x 6in (15.2cm) long cut on the bias
- Machine sewing thread to match fabrics
- Fusible web
- Seam sealant liquid
- Easily removable fabric marker

Making the Reverse Appliqué Flower

1 Use the templates given at the end of the project. Trace the reverse appliqué pattern on to a 3½in (8.9cm) square of fusible web (I used Steam-A-Seam), on the side that has the web attached. Cut the shape out on the line leaving a flower-shaped hole in the centre. Peel the backing paper off and iron the web side of the fusible web on to the wrong side of the fabric you are using for the outside of the flower.

2 Apply a drop of seam sealant (such as Fray Check) to each inside and outside point. Cut the fabric about ¼in (6mm) away from the edge of the fusible web flower (Fig 1). Clip the inside points and the sharp inside curves.

Fig 1

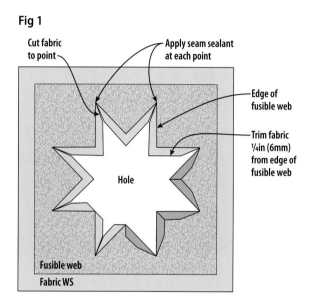

3 Turn the raw edges over the edge of the fusible web (see Turning Raw Edges to the Wrong Side, step 3 in General Techniques). Remove the backing paper carefully and press the edges back over the web, ironing only the very edge (otherwise the web will stick to the iron!).

4 Press a 4in (10.2cm) square of the 'window' fabric to the back of the flower shape, so that the right side of the fabric shows through the window. Iron in place. Machine appliqué around the shape using a blind hem or buttonhole stitch.

Making the Six-Petal Flower

5 Draw around the template for the six-petal flower on the wrong side of a 4in (10.2cm) square of your chosen fabric (see Copying a Template). Place another 4in (10.2cm) square of the same fabric underneath, with right sides facing. Sew on the drawn line and then trim the seam allowance close to the stitching.

6 Apply seam sealant to the inside points before clipping in. Cut a small slit in the centre of the back fabric. Turn the shape through to the right side (see Turning Shapes to the Right Side) and then press.

7 Sew a machine gathering stitch across the flower, length 3.0, from each indent to the opposite indent (see template). Secure the threads at the beginning but not at the end and leave thread tails for pulling up. Pull up the gathering threads at the end of each line, knot and bury them. Sew the flower to the centre of the reverse appliqué flower at each indent between the petals.

Making the Ruched Flower

8 Cut a bias strip of fabric 1¼in x 6in (3.2cm x 15.2cm). Thread your machine with the bobbin thread matching the fabric and the top thread either slightly lighter or slightly darker. This will make it easier when you need to find the correct thread to pull up for gathering. On the wrong side of your fabric, beginning ½in (1.3cm) from one short end, sew a gathering stitch, length 3.5, ¼in (6mm) from the long edge. Stop ½in (1.3cm) from the other short end. Leave thread tails for pulling up the stitches and make sure you don't fix the ends (Fig 2). Press the other long edge to the stitching line, wrong sides together.

Fig 2

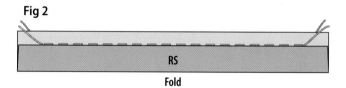

9 Use an easily removable fabric marker to make dots along the folded edge. From the raw edge at the side mark ½in (1.3cm), 1½in (3.8cm), 2½in (6.3cm), 3½in (8.9cm), 4½in (11.4cm) and 5½in (14cm). Along the raw edge, under the stitching, mark 1in (2.5cm), 2in (5.1cm), 3in (7.6cm), 4in (10.2cm) and 5in (12.7cm). Join the dots, alternating between the top and bottom ones to form a zigzag (Fig 3). Sew a gathering stitch, length 3.5 on the line, pivoting at the points. Don't worry about going off the edge. Leave thread tails and don't fix the ends. Pull the bobbin thread to gather the zigzags and form the petal shapes. Knot and bury the thread ends.

Fig 3

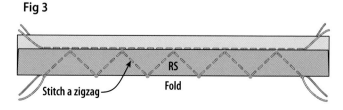

10 Bring the short ends together, right sides facing. The raw edge below the first gathering line will be on the outside. Sew the ends together, ½in (1.3cm) in from the edge, in line with the indent of the first petal (Fig 4). When doing this, start in the middle of the seam and sew towards the petal edge, stopping with the needle down. Pivot the fabric and sew to the other edge. Pivot again and sew back to the middle. This gives a much cleaner finish at the edges. Cut off the thread tails. Turn the shape right side out. Open the seam and trim if necessary. Tidy up all the loose ends except for the original gathering thread tails.

Fig 4

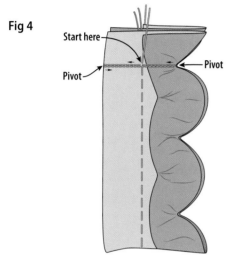

11 Knot the two top thread tails together that are on the inside of the flower and pull up the bobbin threads that are on the outside. Thread them to the inside and knot them. Leave the long ends for sewing the flower to the background. Rub the raw edges of the fabric to fray them and create a tufted centre. Finish by sewing the flower to the centre at each indent between the petals.

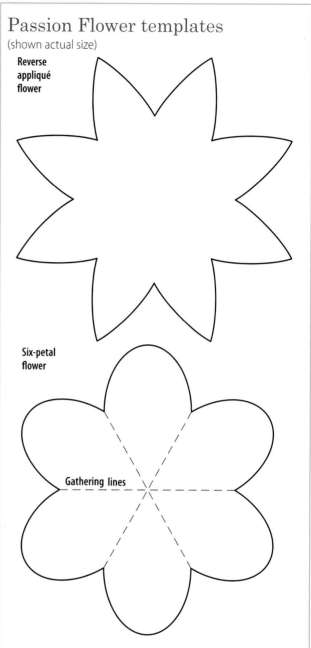

Passion Flower templates
(shown actual size)

Reverse appliqué flower

Six-petal flower

Gathering lines

Design Inspirations...

Made by Sandra Pirie

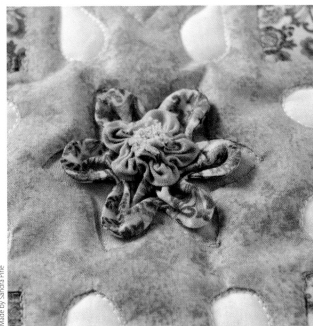

Made by Sallie Hopper

This was one of the flowers I 'christened' after it was made so you will have to stretch your imagination a little! It is made with three flowers in one and so gives the opportunity for using different coloured fabrics for each section, as these pretty examples show.

I used just one passion flower in the centre of my Hawaiian block to add some dimension and colour interest to a relatively simple design. If you would like to make this block, the pattern is available separately – see Suppliers.

Primrose

The primrose is a much-loved flower, with its pretty petals and delicate scent so welcome in the spring after a long winter. The flower I've created here is more representational than realistic so colourwise anything goes. You could stay with the traditional soft yellow of wild primroses or chose more vibrant shades, such as those seen in polyanthus. The ruched flower is topped with an attractive fabric-covered button.

REQUIREMENTS
- Background fabric, size according to your quilt block or project
- Fabric for flower 6in x 1½in (15.2cm x 3.8cm) cut on the bias
- Machine sewing thread to match fabric
- Tiny covered button or similar (optional)

Making the Flower

1 Cut a bias strip 6in x 1½in (15.2cm x 3.8cm). On the wrong side, mark a line ½in (1.3cm) from one long edge. Fold the raw edge to the line, wrong sides together, giving a ¼in (6mm) turning. Iron in place. Bring the opposite raw edge down to the fold along the bottom and iron (see Fig 1). Along the bottom edge mark every 1in (2.5cm), beginning at the end on the left. Along the top edge, mark ½in (1.3cm) from the end on the left and then mark every 1in (2.5cm). Your last mark along the top should be ½in (1.3cm) from the end on the right. Join the marks, forming a zigzag line.

Fig 1

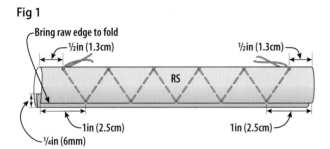

2 Machine a gathering stitch (length 3.0 and tension lowered slightly) along the line. Because the strip is so narrow, an open-toe foot would probably not work too well, so use a regular stitching foot. Pull up the bobbin threads and knot the ends securely. One edge will have five petals, the other four petals (Fig 2).

Fig 2

3 Bring the front sides together (the side that does not have the raw edge at the bottom) so the raw edges at the ends are even. Sew a diagonal line from the end of the fifth petal at the top to the end of the fourth petal at the bottom (Fig 3). The seam will be on the same diagonal as the last line of gathering. To avoid thread tails at the ends, begin in the centre of the diagonal line and sew to the top edge, turn the fabric around and sew to the bottom edge. Turn it around again and then sew back to the centre.

Fig 3

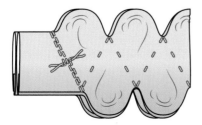

4 Flatten the shape out into a flower with five petals on the outside and four on the inside. Trim the seams a little. The seam edges can be turned under when the flowers are sewn to the background after quilting.

5 To finish, sew a tiny covered button in the centre if desired. Alternatively, you could make a frayed centre – refer to the Marigold chapter for instructions (steps 6 and 7). See the Leaves chapter for ideas on leaves to accompany this flower.

Design Inspirations...

Made by Sallie Hopper

Made by Sandra Pirie

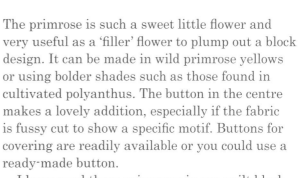

The primrose is such a sweet little flower and very useful as a 'filler' flower to plump out a block design. It can be made in wild primrose yellows or using bolder shades such as those found in cultivated polyanthus. The button in the centre makes a lovely addition, especially if the fabric is fussy cut to show a specific motif. Buttons for covering are readily available or you could use a ready-made button.

I have used three primroses in my quilt block, and along with some clusters of plump pale pink berries they provide a lovely contrast to the more ornate fuchsia flowers. The additional of some simple leaves and curling tendrils completes the block design.

Rose

What book on flowers would be complete without the rose, that perpetual favourite, both in the garden and in the world of art and design. This three-dimensional fabric rose is quite straightforward to make using templates and fusible web. I used a lighter shade for the outside petals and a darker shade for the inner petals to create more depth and realism to the design. A little rosebud is described in the next chapter.

REQUIREMENTS
- Background fabric, size according to your quilt block or project
- Fabric for the rose about 10in (25.4cm) square (see step 5)
- Fabric for the stem 1in x 5in (2.5cm x 12.7cm) cut on the bias
- Fabric for the leaves about 3in (7.6cm) square
- Machine sewing thread to match fabrics
- Soft wool (yarn) to stuff the stem
- Fusible web
- Scrap of wadding (batting)
- Point turner or similar
- Tracing paper
- Tear-away stabilizer
- Water-soluble stabilizer (optional)

Making the Stem

1 From your stem fabric cut a bias strip 1in x 5in (2.5cm x 12.7cm). Refer to Making Bias Stems in the General Techniques section to make the stem. Blind hem stitch the stem in place on your background fabric (see Blind Hem Stitching Appliqué). Stuff the stem with one strand of wool (yarn).

Making the Leaves

2 On fusible web (I used Steam-A-Seam), draw around each leaf template (provided at the end of the chapter) on to the paper side that has the web attached. Cut each leaf out on the line. Peel off the backing paper that wasn't drawn on and iron the fusible web leaves to the wrong side of your leaf fabric. Cut the fabric about ¼in (6mm) from the edge of the fusible web for each leaf. Turn the edges over the fusible web edge (see step 3 of Turning Raw Edges to the Wrong Side). Peel off the backing paper and iron or finger press the edge over.

3 Tack (baste) each leaf to a piece of wadding (batting) and then trim the wadding just under the edge of the leaf. Appliqué the leaves in position on your background fabric using the blind hem stitch or buttonhole appliqué stitch. Sew a triple stitch down the centre of each leaf to represent the vein. Remove the tacking (basting) stitches.

 Tip If you don't have a triple stitch on your machine, then you could sew two rows of straight stitches on top of each other or use two threads through the needle. Both of these methods will give a more pronounced line than a single straight stitch.

Making the Rose Petals

4 Start by making the nine petals. I used a lighter shade for the petals on the outside of the flower (numbers 1, 2, 3, 4 and 5) and a darker shade for the centre petals (numbers 6, 7, 8 and 9). Draw around each petal shape on the wrong side of your fabric – refer to Copying a Template. Place another piece of the same fabric beneath, right sides together, and sew on the line, leaving a gap at the bottom edge of each petal except petal 9. Sew this all the way around and make a slit in the back for turning through.

5 Trim the fabric about 3/16in (5mm) from the sewing line and clip all curves and points. Turn each petal through to the right side – see Turning Shapes to the Right Side. Use a point turner or similar on the inside of the seam to define the edges and then iron each petal flat.

6 Now make the centre. Draw around the template for the rose centre on the wrong side of the fabric and cut out on the line. Fold wrong sides together along the fold line marked on the pattern (Fig 1). With the inside of the rose centre facing up and the fold along the top, mark the curved edge at the bottom in thirds (points B and C on Fig 1). Fold corner A over the shape to point C and then fold corner D to point B (Fig 2). Pin in place and with tear-away stabilizer underneath, sew across the base with a straight stitch, length 2.5. Secure the threads at both ends.

Fig 1

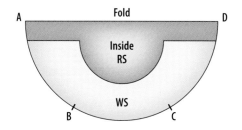

Fig 2

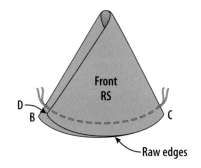

7 Fold the centre in half with the backs facing and sew two stitches, length 3.0, at right angles to the base, about 1/4in (6mm) from the folded edge at the side (Fig 3). Secure the threads at both ends. It is easier if you place a scrap of tear-away stabilizer underneath before you sew. Press this small box pleat flat and trim the corners at the base. If desired, you could place tear-away stabilizer underneath and a water-soluble stabilizer (such as Solvy) on top, to prevent the pleat from moving in front of the needle. Sew across the base, securing the box pleat flat (Fig 4).

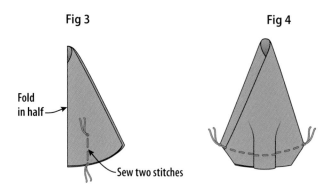

Fig 3   **Fig 4**

Fold in half →

— Sew two stitches

8 Draw Rose Pattern A (shown at the end of the chapter) on to a 4in (10.2cm) square of tracing paper and place this in position on the background fabric where your rose will go. Pin along the top edge of the paper, through to the background. This will be used as a pattern for placing the petals. Place petals 1, 2, 3, 4 and 5 in position on the background, under the tracing paper. Lift up the paper each time to pin the top of the petals to the background. Using a small zigzag stitch, sew the petals in order, lifting the one next to the one being sewn up and out of the way. Sew the lower sides and base of each petal, not the top parts. When the rose is finished, none of this stitching should be showing.

9 Now draw Rose Pattern B on a second 4in (10.2cm) square of tracing paper. Remove Rose Pattern A and replace with Rose Pattern B. Pin and sew petals 6, 7 and 8 in the same way. You could put a small tuck at the base of the petals as you sew them to make them turn up a little at the top. Place the centre in position and sew across the base. Place petal 9 over the centre and blind hem stitch in position. If any of the stitching at the base of the petals is showing, hand sew the backs of petals 6, 7 and 8 to the petals underneath.

Rose templates
(shown actual size)

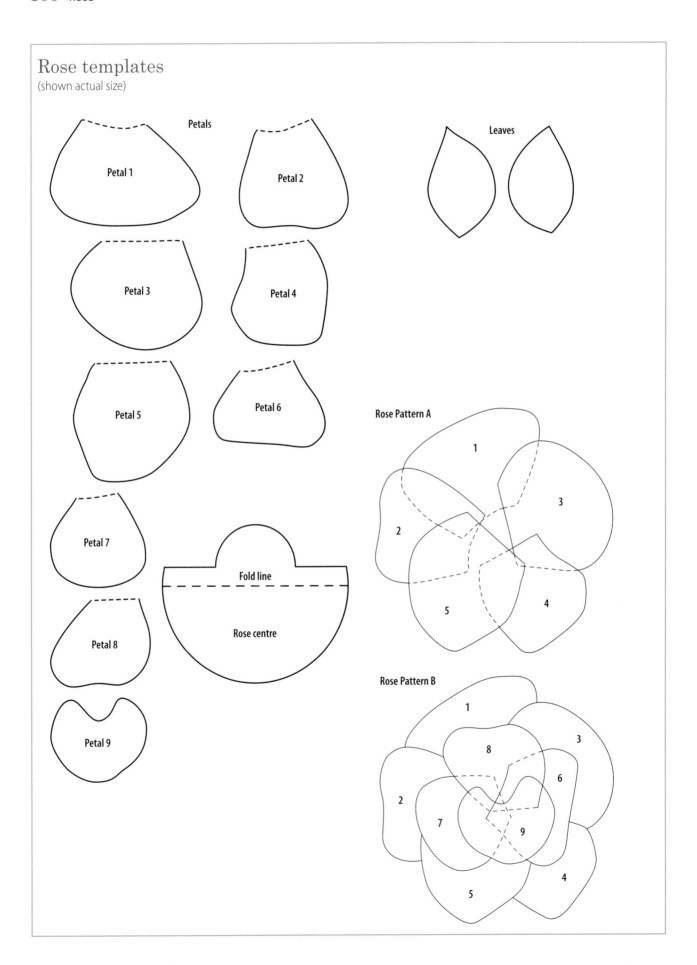

Petals

Petal 1

Petal 2

Leaves

Petal 3

Petal 4

Petal 5

Petal 6

Rose Pattern A

Petal 7

Fold line

Rose centre

Petal 8

Petal 9

Rose Pattern B

Design Inspirations...

Made by Sandra Pirie

Made by Katie George

Roses are perennial favourites and this densely petalled design lends itself to all sorts of fabric colour combinations. Having a slightly darker colour for the inner petals does give the flower more depth, as you can see by these examples.

My quilt block features three roses branching off a central stem, with pairs of leaves, some smooth-edged and some curvy, adorning the stem. Little cream rosebuds help to fill out the design.

Rosebud

A simple little rosebud is a perfect companion to the rose described in the previous chapter. These small budding flowers are useful as accents on a quilt block design, to bring balance or symmetry if desired. They are also excellent for introducing splashes of colour to link different blocks together. Plain fabrics work well, as do prints with tiny motifs.

REQUIREMENTS

- Background fabric, size according to your quilt block or project
- Fabric for the rosebud about 3in (7.6cm) square
- Fabric for the calyx about 3in (7.6cm) square
- Fabric for the stem 1in x 5in (2.5cm x 12.7cm) cut on the bias
- Machine sewing thread to match fabrics
- Soft wool (yarn) to stuff the stem
- Fusible web
- Tear-away stabilizer
- Water-soluble stabilizer (optional)
- Seam sealant liquid

Making the Stem

1 From stem fabric cut a bias strip 1in x 5in (2.5cm x 12.7cm) and make and stuff the stem as described in step 1 of the Rose.

Making the Rosebud

2 Cut out a 2¼in (5.7cm) diameter circle from your rosebud fabric. At the centre on the wrong side, mark the straight grains with ½in (1.3cm) lines using an easily removable marker (see Fig 1). Fold the circle in half, wrong sides together, along the bias grain. With the fold along the top, move the lower edge of the top fabric up so that in the middle it is slightly less than ¼in (6mm) above the fabric underneath. Iron the new fold at the top. This forms the inside of the bud (Fig 2).

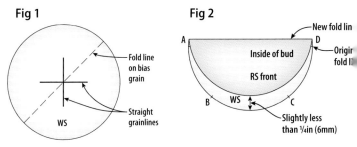

Fig 1

Fold line on bias grain

Straight grainlines

WS

Fig 2

New fold lin

A D

Inside of bud

Origin fold l

RS front

B WS C

Slightly less than ¼in (6mm)

3 At the folded edge, turn back ⅛in (3mm) to the outside of the bud and finger press in place (Fig 3). Place the shape with the inside of the bud uppermost and the fold at the top. Mark the curved edge at the bottom in thirds (points B and C on Fig 2). Open out the ⅛in (3mm) turning at corner A, fold this corner over the shape to point C and pin in place (Fig 4). Now open out the ⅛in (3mm) turning at corner D and fold this corner over the shape to point B (Fig 5). Turn under ⅛in (3mm) to the inside at corner D (Fig 6) and pin in place. With tear-away stabilizer underneath, sew across the base of the bud with a straight stitch, length 2.5. Secure the threads at both ends.

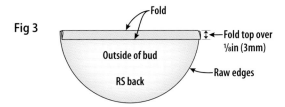

Fig 3

Fold

Outside of bud

Fold top over ⅛in (3mm)

Raw edges

RS back

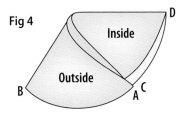

Fig 4

D

Inside

Outside

B A C

Fig 5

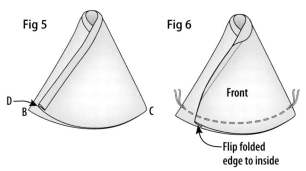

Fig 6

Front

Flip folded edge to inside

Making the Calyx

5 On fusible web, draw around the calyx template and cut it out on the line. Peel off the backing paper and iron the web side to the wrong side of your calyx fabric.

Tip If you find the calyx shape a little too fiddly then you could use the petal 9 template of the Rose instead.

4 Fold the bud in half with the backs facing and sew two stitches, length 3.0, at right angles to the base, about ¼in (6mm) from the folded edge at the side (Fig 7). This forms a pleat and makes the base small enough to sit in the calyx. Secure the threads at both ends. Press this small box pleat flat and trim the corners of the bud at the base. Place tear-away stabilizer underneath and a water-soluble stabilizer (if needed) on top to prevent the pleat from moving in front of the needle. Sew across the base of the bud, securing the box pleat flat (Fig 8). Remove both stabilizers. Place the bud in position on your background (use fabric glue to hold it) and sew a small zigzag stitch along the base and ¼in (6mm) up both sides to secure.

6 Trim the fabric about ³⁄₁₆in (5mm) from the edge of the fusible web. Apply seam sealant to each inside point and when dry, clip these points to the edge of the fusible web. Turn the raw edges over the edges of the web (see step 3 of Turning Raw Edges to the Wrong Side). Make sure the shape looks fairly symmetrical from the front before removing the backing paper from the web and ironing the edges in place.

7 To finish, blind hem stitch or hand sew the calyx in place all around the edge (use fabric glue to hold in position) so that it covers the base of the rosebud.

Fig 7

Fold in half → Front

Sew two stitches

Fig 8

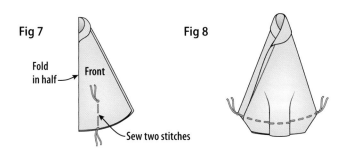

Rosebud template
(shown actual size)

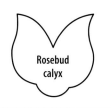

Rosebud calyx

Design Inspirations...

Rosebuds can be made in any colour you choose, and with plain or print fabrics. Apart from making rosebuds to accompany full roses, the small finished size makes buds ideal as 'fillers', useful for extending a design.

In my quilt block featuring roses, little rosebuds burst from a secondary curving design. I made these buds using a cream fabric but delicate multicolour batiks would also look wonderful.

Made by Sallie Hopper

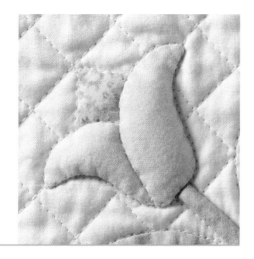

Tulip

The tulip is a fabulous flower and has been popular for centuries. It grows in many shapes, from elegant lily-flowered to flamboyant parrots and is available in many gorgeous colours. I've chosen a simple shape that only needs three petal templates to create a lovely tulip flower. The flower head is balanced by some easy leaves and a single stem. The tulip with a pair of leaves looks good on its own and also as a symmetrical group.

REQUIREMENTS
- Background fabric, size according to your quilt block or project
- Fabric for the petals about 4in x 3in (10.2cm x 7.6cm)
- Fabric for the bud about 2in (5.1cm) square
- Fabric for the leaves about 4in x 5in (10.2cm x 12.7cm)
- Fabric for the stem 4in x 1¼in (10.2cm x 3.2cm) cut on the bias
- Machine sewing thread to match fabrics
- Fusible web and medium weight fusible interfacing
- Soft wool (yarn) to stuff the stem
- Small amount of toy stuffing
- Seam sealant liquid

Making the Leaves

1 Use the templates provided at the end of the chapter. Draw around the leaf template on to fusible web (I used Steam-A-Seam) and cut it out on the line. Peel the backing paper off the fusible web and place the shape, web side down, on the wrong side of the fabric you have chosen for the leaves. Press with an iron to fuse. Cut the fabric about ¼in (6mm) from the edge of the fusible web. Place a drop of seam sealant (such as Fray Check) at the tip of each leaf and also at the V at the top of the stem – see Fig 1.

Fig 1

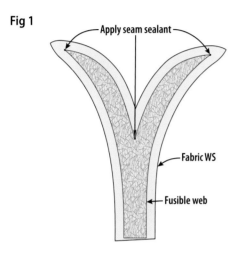

2 Clip the fabric at the V, right up to the edge of the fusible web (Fig 2). Turn the fabric over the edges of the fusible web (see step 3 of Turning Raw Edges to the Wrong Side). Carefully remove the backing paper from the fusible web and press the edges down again, keeping the points sharp. Iron the leaf shapes on to your background fabric and blind hem stitch in place.

Fig 2

Making the Stem

3 From your stem fabric cut a bias strip 4in x 1¼in (10.2cm x 3.2cm). On the right side, mark a line from one long edge, ⅜in (1cm) at the top tapering to ¼in (6mm) at the bottom. Fold wrong sides together with the marked line on the top. Sew along the line. Iron the seam allowance open, placing it in the centre of the stem. Trim the seam allowances close to the seam.

4 Pin or stick (using a fabric glue stick) the stems in position on the background, with the wider end at the base and the seam underneath. Select the built-in blind hem stitch on your machine and do not alter the settings. Attach the blind hem foot that came with your machine and sew down the right-hand side of the stem without securing the stitches at the beginning or the end. The point of the zigzag should just pierce the side of the stem and the straight stitches will be on the background fabric only (Fig 3). These stitches will be removed later and are only to keep the stem in place temporarily.

Fig 3

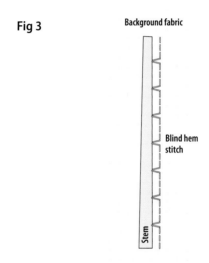

5 On the left side of the stem, fold back the edge so that it just covers the raw edge of the seam allowance (see Fig 4). Sew this edge only with your appliqué setting blind hem stitch, using an open-toe foot. Secure the ends. Remove the first blind hem stitching. Fold back this side of the stem so that it just covers the raw edge of the seam allowance and blind hem appliqué stitch in place. Now stuff the stem with two strands of wool (yarn). You should have a raised and rounded stem.

Fig 4

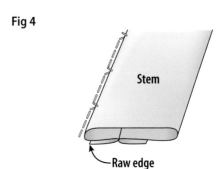

Making the Petals

6 Using the template provided, draw around the bud shape on the wrong side of your bud fabric (see Copying a Template in the General Techniques section). Place the non-sticky side of a piece of medium weight fusible interfacing on to the right side of the fabric and sew on the line, leaving the base open (see step 1 of Turning Raw Edges to the Wrong Side). Trim the seam allowance and turn the shape through to the right side. Repeat for the smaller petal shape.

7 Make the larger petal shape in the same way but sew around the complete shape, make a slit in the interfacing and turn the shape through to the right side through the slit (see Turning Shapes to the Right Side). Press all the shapes flat.

8 Using the placement guide, place the open end of the small petal under the edge of the large petal and pin the bud underneath. Make sure it is in the centre and lines up with the pattern. Using a blind hem stitch, sew the top of the small petal to the bud (Fig 5). Sew the larger petal from the edge of the bud all the way to the base of the two petals. Blind hem stitch the tulip to the background, bringing the sides in slightly for stuffing (see Blind Hem Stitching Appliqué).

Fig 5

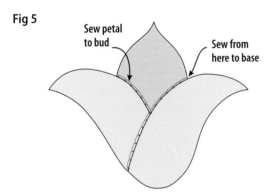

Sew petal to bud

Sew from here to base

9 Make a small slit in the background fabric behind the tulip and push a small amount of toy stuffing through the gap to pad the tulip. Hand sew the slit closed. To finish, sew a straight stitch in the seam ditches (Fig 6).

Fig 6

After stuffing sew along the dashed lines

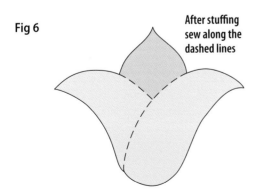

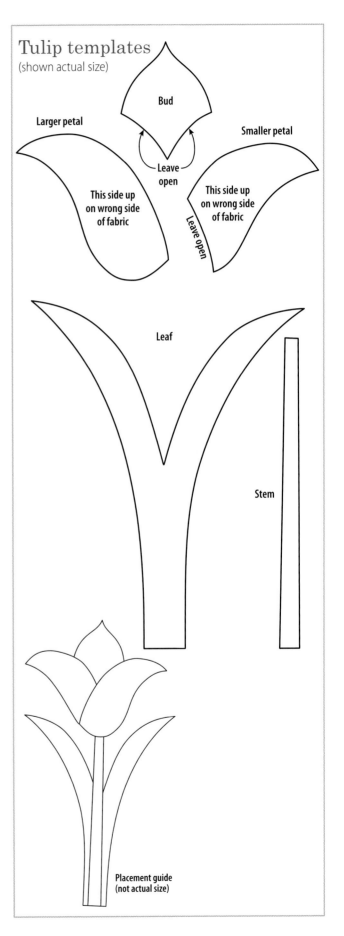

Tulip templates
(shown actual size)

Bud

Larger petal

Smaller petal

Leave open

This side up on wrong side of fabric

Leave open

This side up on wrong side of fabric

Leaf

Stem

Placement guide (not actual size)

Design Inspirations...

Made by Katie George

Made by Sallie Hopper

This tulip is so easy to make and yet so effective you are sure to want to include it in many of your projects. The flower looks lovely in plain fabrics or those with a small print but can also be given a modern twist with bolder prints or batiks, as the example here shows.

I used the tulip with leaves in a symmetrical arrangement in my quilt block and alternated them with clematis flowers. A large chrysanthemum flower in the centre hides all the ends of the stems and provides a focal point.

Leaves

If you want to make a quilt or other project using blocks created from the flowers described in this book you may also need a variety of leaf shapes to add to your flowers. Some of the flower chapters already have instructions for leaves but this short section gives more ideas and some template shapes you could use.

REQUIREMENTS
- Fabric for leaves
- Machine sewing thread to match fabrics
- Fusible web
- Wadding (batting)
- Seam sealant liquid

SINGLE LEAVES

Single leaves are very useful for flowers such as the lily of the valley, rose, pansy and primrose and a selection of different leaves are given in Fig 1 for you to enlarge to the size you require. Leaves on their own can be made to branch out from a stem on alternate sides, such as on the primroses and bell flowers.

Single leaves can be made as mirror-image pairs, placed on either side of the stem or at the base of a flower stem, as in the begonia flowers.

Single leaves can also be arranged with stems to form a spray of leaves, as seen in the foxglove and gerbera block.

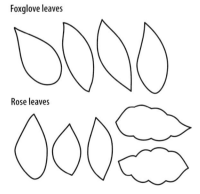

Fig 1
Enlarge these leaf templates to the size required

Foxglove leaves

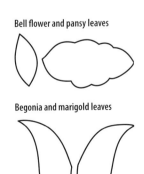

Rose leaves

Bell flower and pansy leaves

Begonia and marigold leaves

Fuchsia and primrose leaves

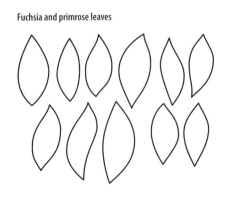

Making Single Leaves

I used two different methods for leaves. In Method 1 leaves have a raw edge and are appliquéd with a satin stitch. In Method 2 they have turned edges and are appliquéd with a blind hem stitch.

Method 1

1 Draw the leaf template on to fusible web (I used Steam-A-Seam), on the backing paper with web attached. Roughly cut around the outside of the drawing. Peel off the backing paper not drawn on and place the leaf, web side down, on the wrong side of the fabric, preferably on the bias grain. Press with an iron and then cut the leaf out on the line.

2 On the background fabric, mark the placement of the leaf. Remove the backing paper, iron it in place and machine satin stitch, width 2.0, around the edge (see Satin Stitching in General Techniques). If you are adding veins on your leaf, sew these at this point using a triple stitch or a straight stitch with two top threads in the needle.

Method 2

1 Trace the leaf template on to fusible web and then cut it out on the line. Peel off the backing paper and iron the leaf to the wrong side of the fabric. Cut the fabric about ³⁄₁₆in (5mm) from the edge of the fusible web. If the leaf edge has indents then place a drop of seam sealant at each indent and when dry, clip the fabric right up to the point of each indent.

2 Turn the edges over the fusible web – refer to Turning Raw Edges to the Wrong Side. Remove the second backing paper and press the edges again.

3 Pin and tack (baste) the shape to a piece of wadding (batting) and trim the wadding away just under the edges of the leaf. Blind hem stitch the leaf to the background (see Blind Hem Stitching Appliqué). Sew a triple stitch down the leaf centre for a vein.

GROUPED LEAVES

For blocks that have a symmetrical design, such as the bells, pansy and lily block shown here, a cluster of leaves in a symmetrical grouping is useful to act as a base to the design.

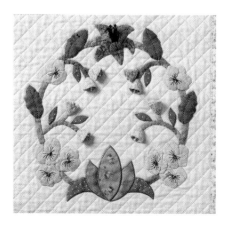

Making Grouped Leaves

1 Fig 2A shows the finished leaf cluster. Enlarge the templates to the size you require. Trace the individual shapes for the leaf cluster, given in Fig 2B (the centre leaf, leaf A, leaf B, leaf C and leaf D) on fusible web (I used Steam-A-Seam), on the side that has the web attached and roughly cut them out. Peel off the backing paper that is not drawn on and iron the shapes to the wrong side of the fabric. Cut the shapes out on the line.

2 Peel off the second backing paper and place leaf A and leaf B on the background first. Satin stitch them to the background, width 2.0. Next place leaves C and D in position and satin stitch in place. Finally, satin stitch the centre leaf on top of leaves C and D.

Fig 4A
Enlarge templates to size required

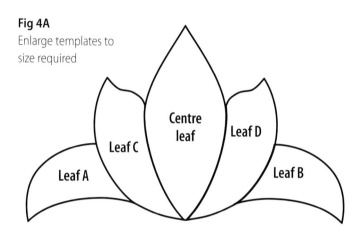

Fig 4B

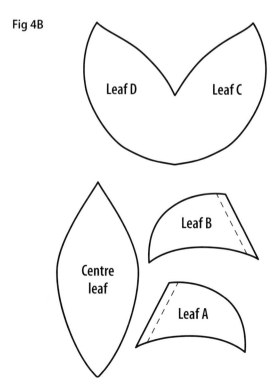

General Techniques

This section describes how to do the general techniques that are common to many of the flowers in the book, including making bias stems, satin stitching appliqué edges and blind hem stitching.

COPYING A TEMPLATE

Templates are provided full size at the end of the relevant project. Sometimes it is possible to see through your fabric sufficiently to copy a template but if not the usual way to transfer a shape on to the fabric is to draw it on to template plastic, cut it out and draw round the plastic shape on to your background. However, a much easier way is to copy the shape on to tear-away stabilizer. Place the stabilizer on the wrong side of your fabric, stitch on the line and then tear off the stabilizer.

There is a small consideration with this method though. When drawing round a template, the line will be a little outside the exact size of the template. This is good! Turning the shape through to the right side after it has been sewn makes it that little bit smaller, making it about the same size as the original. If you sew on the exact template line on the tear-away stabilizer, your shape will be a little smaller than the original. In other words, when using tear-away stabilizer, you will need to sew a fraction outside the line!

USING FUSIBLE WEB

Fusible web is made up of an ultra-thin sheet of adhesive backed with a special paper. When the web is placed between two fabrics the heat of an iron causes the adhesive to melt and fuse the fabrics together. Various manufacturers produce fusible webs and the specific type you use may depend on what is available in your area and your experience of using a particular brand. The most common ones are Steam-A-Seam and Bondaweb (also known as Vliesofix in Europe and Wonder Under in the USA). I have used Steam-A-Seam2 for the flowers in this book, which has two paper backings. Bondaweb only has one backing, so when using this product you will need to change your method slightly, consulting the manufacturer's instructions if necessary. I've used Steam-A-Seam as a base for turning raw edges to the wrong side and in these cases Bondaweb is *not* a suitable substitute as the paper backing is not firm enough.

MAKING BIAS STEMS

These are used on many of the flowers in different widths and lengths. Some are stuffed with cord, soft wool (yarn) or wadding (batting) while others are left flat. Because the strips usually need to bend and stretch around curves, they are cut on the bias grain of the fabric, which is more stretchy. Quite short lengths are needed, so start at one corner of your fabric rather than cutting diagonally from one long edge. There are different ways of making bias stems and I think I have tried them all! The method I prefer is to use bias bars when possible. These are heatproof and are therefore safe to use with an iron. Cut the width of the strips twice the finished width required plus ½in (1.3cm).

1 Start by cutting the strips the required width and length along the bias grain (see Fig 1A, B, C, D).

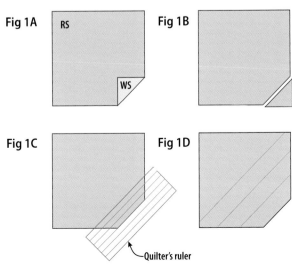

Fig 1A — RS / WS

Fig 1B

Fig 1C

Fig 1D — Quilter's ruler

2 Gently fold the strip in half lengthways, wrong sides together, without stretching the folded edge. Using a 4.0 stitch length machine ¼in (6mm) from the raw edges. As a guide, draw a line and adjust the needle ¼in (6mm) from the edge of the foot. Alternatively, line the raw edges along the edge of a ¼in-foot. If your fabric is out of control because it is thin and on the bias, then place a piece of tear-away stabilizer underneath and rip it away after the seam has been sewn.

3 If you have a small enough bias bar, insert this through the stem with the seam running along the centre of the flat edge of the bar. Press the seam open with an iron. If the bar is too wide, place the seam in the centre of the strip and open it using your thumbs before pressing with an iron.

4 Keeping the bias bar in place (if used) trim the seam allowance next to the stitching line. Remove the bias bar and iron the strip again, keeping the seam down the centre. Trim off any loose threads that may show from the right side.

Fig 2

Fig 3

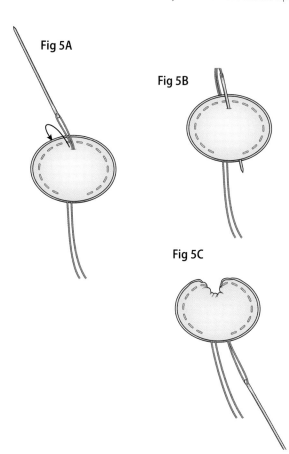

Bias bar

Fig 4

TURNING SHAPES TO THE RIGHT SIDE

Some of the petals of the appliqué flowers are quite small and can be a little tricky to turn through to the right side. I have developed a method that makes the process a little easier. A needle gripper is also useful – see Materials and Equipment. It is best to shorten the stitch length when sewing small shapes. This will result in smoother curves and help prevent the raw edges from poking through after the shape is turned through to the right side.

1 Thread a needle (one that doesn't have a sharp point) with a length of sewing thread, about 10in (25.4cm) and bring the two ends together. Insert the point of the needle between the two fabrics of the shape through the unsewn opening. Bring it out at the top of the shape through the front fabric, just below the stitching (Fig 5A).

2 Take the needle over the top of the shape and then insert it at the top of the shape in the back fabric, just below the stitching. Bring the needle out through the gap at the bottom (Fig 5B). Pull all the threads to bring the top part of the shape to the inside and then out through the gap at the bottom (Fig 5C). Remove the needle and thread and it will be ready to use on the next shape.

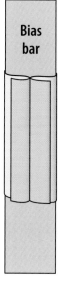

Fig 5A

Fig 5B

Fig 5C

BLIND HEM STITCHING APPLIQUE

This is one of the two main stitches I use for appliqué and the other is buttonhole stitch. Both are found on most modern machines although some width and length adjustments have to be made to the blind hem stitch function. The stitch looks like Fig 6A but the length and width both need to be made smaller so it looks more like Fig 6B.

Fig 6A   **Fig 6B**

On some machines, when you adjust the width, it will move the stitch over to the left or right instead of narrowing the zigzag. If this is the case, then there is usually a picot edge stitch which is a blind hem stitch with the zigzag pointing to the right instead of the left. The width of this can usually be adjusted and then you will need to mirror image it or sew with the appliqué on the right of the needle instead of the left.

To achieve the best adjustment, you will need to make a sample. Use two small pieces of fabric and fold an edge of one piece under and put it on top of the second piece to create a folded edge to be appliquéd on to a background (see Fig 7). The straight stitches of the stitch pattern should be on the background fabric, right next to the folded edge. The point of the zigzag should just pierce the folded edge. Adjust the stitch to the smallest width you can without missing the edge. Adjust the length so that the total length of the straight stitches is about ⅜in (1cm). All machines are different: some give the length of each stitch (which will be about 1.5), while others give the length of the complete pattern. Some have four straight stitches, others three or five, so you will have to experiment to find the best adjustment for your machine.

Fig 7

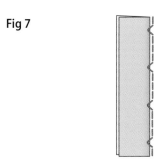

The buttonhole appliqué stitch can also be used. This is similar in that the straight stitches should be in the background very close to the appliqué fabric edge and the horizontal stitch piercing the appliqué. A tiny zigzag stitch also works well.

Use an open-toe foot on your machine for most of your appliqué. If you find that the points are not staying down when you come to sew them, or your appliqué shape is very narrow, such as a stem, then try a clear embroidery foot (*not* a free-motion darning foot). As this doesn't have a large gap in front, it will keep the fabric more secure.

Needles and Threads for Appliqué

Because a Universal needle goes into the fabric between the fibres, the stitch may look a little distorted, in which case use a Microtex Sharp 70/10 needle. This will pierce through the fibres rather than sink between them, giving a more precise stitch.

I like to use a thread that matches the appliqué fabric, although in some cases I've found that a thread to match the background is better. Fine silk threads are lovely but the colour choice is limited. Many people are fans of monofilament thread but I very rarely use it. It does give a more invisible look, but that isn't always what I am trying to achieve. I quite like the dimpled look of the appliqué edges. To me it makes it look more authentic, but that's my personal choice. If you do decide to use monofilament then make sure you use a good quality one such as YLI or Sulky Gütermann, and use a cotton thread in the bobbin to match your background fabric. If you see the bobbin thread on the top, first make sure you have put the bottom thread through the bobbin hole if applicable and then loosen the top tension (to a lower number). You will need to sew a test piece for each new appliqué to make sure you are using the correct thread and stitch size.

Programming Blind Hem Stitch

If your machine allows you to programme stitches you may be able to do this. There are two types of programmes that can be used. The first and easiest one is to select the stitch, adjust the length and width and then store it in the memory. You could also store a mirror-imaged version so that you have one facing left and the other facing right. A straight stitch in the same menu is also very useful and saves time when going from one to the other.

The second way is a little more technical but if your machine is able to do, it is much easier to use. The advantage is that you can programme two or three small stitches between the zigzags instead of having four minute ones that look too bunched up. On some machines, you can also move the programmed stitch across, so that the straight stitches line up with the centre of the foot.

First you will need to decide the best width and length of your stitch. I have programmed a few into my machine, all with different adjustments, as different appliqué sizes and shapes require different lengths and widths of stitches.

The basic method is to programme two straight stitches (L:2.0) and a zigzag stitch. Adjust the zigzag to the required width and length (L:0.5, W:1.0) and then go back to the straight stitch in front of the zigzag and adjust the position so that it touches the end of the zigzag (W:1.0) – see Fig 8. Now go back and make the same adjustment to the other straight stitch. Before you sew, make sure the stitch is facing the right direction. If not, then select the side-to-side mirror image. Not all machines will have the same length and width recommendations above, but the principle is the same. I normally use a zigzag width of 0.5, but this is dangerously narrow. I have also programmed in one that has three straight

stitches, length 1.5. It is also a good idea to have a left-facing and a right-facing stitch in the programme.

If you are unable to achieve a good looking blind hem stitch, then either use a small zigzag stitch or a buttonhole appliqué stitch, both of which will look fine.

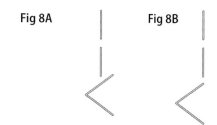

Fig 8A   **Fig 8B**

SATIN STITCHING

This is the usual stitch to sew around a raw edge as the closeness of it prevents the fabric edges from fraying. I've used it to apply appliqué to a background fabric and also as an edging on some free-standing petals, such as the carnation.

Rayon, cotton or polyester thread may be used, depending on the effect you are trying to achieve. Use an open-toe foot unless the points of the appliqué are coming away from the background, in which case use a normal embroidery or crafting foot as this will provide more stability.

Different stitch widths may be used depending on the size of the appliqué. Any width from 2.0–4.0 would be fine. The stitches should be close enough so the appliqué fabric doesn't show through but not so close that it may bunch up and sew on the spot. To give a rounded stitch effect on the top, the tension usually needs to be set a little lower than normal – this is automatically done on most computer machines that have a built-in satin stitch. If your machine has a bobbin case with a hole in the arm of it then the bobbin thread should be placed through this. You don't need to use the same thread in the bobbin as your top thread. A normal machine sewing thread or bobbin thread will work well.

You might need to use a finer needle than usual, a 70/10, because the stitches are so close that with a thicker needle this could weaken the fabric. Because a Universal needle goes into the fabric between the fibres, the stitch may look a little jagged along the edges, in which case, use a Microtex Sharp 70 or 60. This will pierce through the fibres rather than sink between them, giving a straighter edge to the satin stitch.

Sewing Curves

When satin stitching on gradual curves, it's best to guide the fabric smoothly round without pivoting. However, on sharper curves, the needle should be left in the fabric while turning or pivoting. It is important to keep the shape of the curve and stitch without any jagged edges. Figs 9A and 9B show the wrong and right ways to stitch. The golden rules are: On outside curves, stop with needle on the outside of the appliqué edge. On inside curves, stop with needle on the inside of the appliqué edge.

Fig 9B - Outside curves

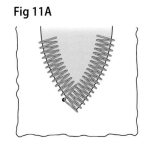

Fig 9B - Inside curves

Sewing Outside Corners

There are a few ways to sew outside corners. The one most people use is, with the appliqué on the left, to satin stitch just over the bottom edge and leave the needle down on the right (the background side). Pivot the fabric and the needle will be at the top edge, above the previous satin stitching, and continue down the next side. The problem with this method is that you are sewing on top of a block of stitching at a corner, which can result in the needle sewing in one spot and the stitching bunching up.

Another method is to mitre the satin stitch as you approach the corner, pivot and mitre again. This sounds perfect but only a few machines will allow you to angle a satin stitch from one side at a time and even then, it is incredibly difficult to make it look even. Added to this you will have a very narrow satin stitch on both sides right at the point.

The following method I think is the best – trust me! Assuming the appliqué is on the left-hand side, sew a few stitches beyond the corner and stop with the needle down on the left (Fig 10A). Lift the presser foot, pivot the fabric and turn the hand wheel towards you until the needle comes out of the fabric and swings over to the right (Fig 10B). Realign the fabric so that the needle goes back down into the same hole it came out of. Lower the presser foot and continue sewing (Fig 10C). The new line of

satin stitching will start directly underneath the previous line. If the appliqué is on the right, stop with the needle on the right. Remember to always stop just past the edge with the needle on the appliqué side.

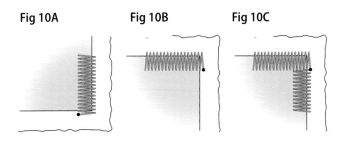

Fig 10A   **Fig 10B**   **Fig 10C**

Sewing Inside Corners

Use the same method as for outside corners, above, but stop just *before* the next edge with the needle in the appliqué. Pivot, realign the needle and continue sewing.

Sewing Points

The method is the same as for sewing corners. The only difference is that as you approach the point, guide your fabric so that the stitch is angled the same as the next edge and turn the point the same way as for corners (Fig 11A and 11B).

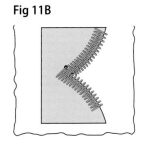

Fig 11A   **Fig 11B**

TURNING RAW EDGES TO THE WRONG SIDE

Satin stitch is the most commonly used stitch for appliquéing a shape that has raw edges as there are no gaps in the stitch to expose the raw edge. However, if the raw edge is turned to the wrong side, there is a wider choice of appliqué stitches that can be used as the shape needs only to be anchored to the background without having to cover the whole edge with stitches. There are various methods of turning the edges over, as follows.

Method 1

1 Draw a mirror image of your shape on the wrong side of the fabric. Place a piece of medium weight fusible interfacing with the non-fusible side facing the right side of the fabric. Stitch on the line (see note at end) and then trim the fabric and interfacing about ⅛in–¼in (3mm–6mm) from the stitching.

2 Make a small slit in the middle of the interfacing and turn the shape through to the right side (see Turning Shapes to the Right Side). Iron the shape flat, making sure none of the interfacing shows on the right side. Note: if you drew around a template to mark your appliqué shape, then stitch on the line. If you traced your shape then stitch a fraction outside the line.

Method 2

Use the same method as above but instead of using fusible interfacing, use a piece of the same fabric (or another fabric if desired), right sides facing. This method is the best for three-dimensional appliqué where both sides of the shape will be seen.

Method 3

1 For the following method fusible web is used as a base for turning the edges (I used Steam-A-Seam). Draw a mirror image of the shape on a piece of fusible web (if using Steam-A-Seam draw on the backing paper that has the web attached). Cut the shape out on the line. Peel off the backing paper that was not drawn on.

2 Place the sticky side of the shape to the wrong side of the fabric and iron to fuse. Trim the fabric about ⅜in (1cm) from the edge of the fusible web. Turn the edges over and on to the fusible web backing paper using method a), b), c) or d) below.
a) Using a glue stick, spread the glue on the fabric edges that do not have the fusible web on. Using your fingernail along the edge of the fusible web and a pointed tool in your other hand (such as tweezers or wooden stick), turn the edge and press it down over the fusible web. Press with a small iron.
b) Instead of a glue stick, use a Clover Fabric Folding Pen along the edge.

c) Squirt some spray starch in a small container and apply this to the fabric edges using a small paintbrush. Use a small iron to turn the edges over the fusible web and press them in position.
d) Make a template from heat-resistant plastic of the appliqué shape (or use a Mylar circle if you are making circles), apply a Clover Fabric Folding Pen to the fabric edge and then a Sewline Glue Stick. Place the template on top of the fusible web and using the side edge of a mini iron or small iron, press the fabric edge over the top of the template. When all the edges have been turned, remove the template plastic and press again.

3 After the edges have been turned, carefully peel off the second backing paper from the fusible web. Iron the turned edge only (any exposed web will stick to the iron!). Your shape is now ready for finishing the edges with a stitch of your choice.

TURNING POINTS AND CURVES

To turn the edges at a point, first apply a drop of seam sealant liquid at the point and when dry fold over one side against the fusible web (Fig 12A and 12B). Next fold over the other side so that at the point the two sides will be overlapping (Fig 12C). Trim off the excess fabric that is protruding at the tip on the right side of the shape (Fig 12D).

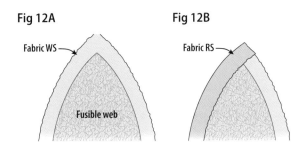

Fig 12A   **Fig 12B**

Fabric WS

Fabric RS

Fusible web

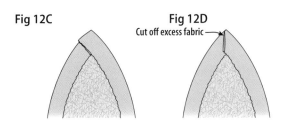

Fig 12C   **Fig 12D**

Cut off excess fabric

Turning Inside Curves and Inside Points

First place a drop of seam sealant such as Fray Check on the fabric next to the edge of the fusible web along the sharp curve or inside point only. When it has dried snip the fabric from the raw edge to the edge of the fusible web. For an inside point you will only need to make one cut but on sharp inside curves you may need to make a few – see Fig 13A. When the edges are turned, the cuts will open out allowing the fabric to lie flat (Fig 13B).

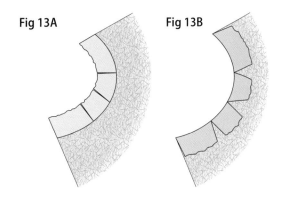

Fig 13A   **Fig 13B**

Turning Outside Curves

When turning the edges around a curve, to eliminate pointy edges, make lots of tiny pleats rather than a few large ones (see Fig 14).

Fig 14

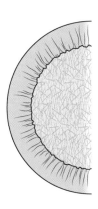

CREATING TENDRILS

I have used two different methods to sew the cord to represent tendrils – couching over cord and chain stitching over cord. You can stick with one method or try both.

Couching

1 Begin sewing the cord to the background at the top of the tendril, leaving a short tail of cord about 1in (2.5cm) long.

2 Select a zigzag stitch and adjust the width so it just covers the thickness of the cord (Fig 15). Couch the cord to the background, turning it around to form the curly shape. You could use a fabric glue pen to hold it in position. Use either a thread that matches the cord or a monofilament thread (you may need to lower the thread tension if using monofilament).

3 Using a hand sewing needle with a large eye, pull the cord ends through to the back, if they are not to be covered by appliqué.

Fig 15

Chain Stitching

1 Cut a length of cord three times the length of the line to be sewn. Fold the cord in half to mark the centre and then open it out straight. Set the machine to stop with the needle in the down position if you can. Secure the cord centre at the top of the line or end of the tendril using a triple stitch (select the 'stop' or 'end of pattern' button to make sure you sew only one) (see Fig 16A). Alternatively, use one straight stitch to secure the cord.

2 Sew one straight stitch, L: 2.5, and stop with the needle in the fabric (Fig 16B). Lift the presser foot and cross the two lengths of cord over in front of the needle, bringing the cord ends straight out to the sides (Fig 16C). Lower the presser foot.

3 Sew two straight stitches and stop with the needle in the fabric. Lift the presser foot and cross the cord in front of needle. Lower the presser foot.

4 Repeat step 3 all the way down the line trying to keep the cord chain tension even (Fig 16D). Stop just before the end of the line. 'Fix' to secure the stitching and cut off the cord ends leaving tails of about 1½in (3.8cm). Using a hand sewing needle with a large eye, pull the cord ends through to the back, if they are not to be covered by appliqué.

Fig 16A   **Fig 16B**

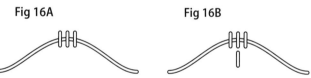

Fig 16C   **Fig 16D**

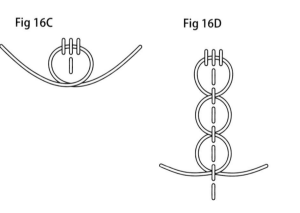

Making a Twisted Cord

You can twist cords either in the same colour or in different colours using the bobbin winder on your machine. The cords will be folded in half at one end so these are perfect for tendrils used on the grape vines as the end will not have to be pulled through to the back. A bead can also be attached at the folded/finished end if desired, as I did for the lily stamens.

1 Cut one or two cords, each at least twice the required finished length. Tie them together at one end. Depending on your machine, either place the ends through the centre hole of a bobbin (Fig 17A) or tie them with a double knot around the middle where the thread is usually wound.

Fig 17A   **Fig 17B**

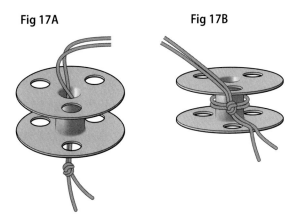

2 Place the bobbin on the bobbin winding spindle, trapping the ends of the cords underneath if you placed the ends through the hole in the centre. If the cords are quite thick and are in the hole of the bobbin, it may be difficult to place the bobbin on the spindle but do not force them. In this case it would be best to tie them around the bobbin (Fig 17B).

3 Engage the bobbin winding function and hold the cords taut. Slowly wind the bobbin (by either pressing the start button or the foot pedal, depending on your machine) and the cords will twist. When they have twisted sufficiently (that is, quite a bit!) stop the machine and still keeping the cords taut with one hand, hold the cords halfway between the bobbin and the ends with the other hand. Again, keeping it taut, bring the ends of the cords to the bobbin, halving the length. Let go of the folded, halfway end of the cords and they will twist against each other.

4 Remove the cords from the bobbin and tie all the ends together. Couch the twisted cord to the background as in described in Couching previously.

Making a Twisted Cord with Bead End

To make the lily stamens with beaded ends, thread a bead on to the cords before they are twisted. Slide the bead down so that it is halfway between the bobbin and the ends of the cords. Twist the cords and hold them at the point where the bead is before bringing the ends to the bobbin as before. You will have twisted cords with a bead at the folded end.

Suppliers

Most of the supplies you will be able to find at your favourite quilt supply store or Pauline's website: www.paulineineson.co.uk The instructions and pattern to make the quilt, Floral Dimensions (including the Celtic, Hawaiian and quilted blocks, the borders and the 'back to front' method of joining the squares) are also available from Pauline's website.

Acknowledgments

So many people supported me in writing this book. Thanks go to all the ladies who attend my courses in Sytchampton, who never cease to encourage, challenge (in the nicest possible way!) and inspire me to create new projects. Many have been coming along for so many years, they are like my extended family.

To Lin Clements and Jeni Hennah at David & Charles for their editorial expertise and Sarah Clark for the lovely book design. To my ever-patient daughters, Laura and Katie, who always give me their honest opinion (whether I want it or not!) when I show them a new design – they are usually right! Last but not least, to my husband, Jim, who has encouraged and supported me throughout, travelled with me to shows, hung quilts, put up stands, sold items he has no idea about and really tried hard to look as though he is interested in this quilting stuff! I am so lucky.

About the Author

Pauline Ineson has been joined at the hip to a sewing machine from a young age. She has explored all forms of machine sewing to include dressmaking, quilting, free motion, heirloom sewing and appliqué, producing many original designs and techniques. Whilst living in America for seventeen years, she ran a very successful sewing school for children. The techniques for the award-winning Heirloom Quilt and Floral Dimensions Quilt are taught by Pauline at Sytchampton near Worcester, where she has been teaching many other machine sewing courses for over ten years.

Index

A DAVID & CHARLES BOOK
© F&W Media International, LTD 2012

David & Charles is an imprint of F&W Media International, LTD
Brunel House, Forde Close, Newton Abbot, TQ12 4PU, UK

F&W Media International, LTD is a subsidiary of F+W Media, Inc.
10151 Carver Road, Suite #200, Blue Ash, OH 45242, USA.

First published in the UK and USA in 2012
Digital edition published in 2012

Text and designs © Pauline Ineson 2012
Layout and photography © F&W Media International, LTD 2012

A catalogue record for this book is available from the British Library.

ISBN-13: 978-1-4463-0181-4 paperback
ISBN-10: 1-4463-0181-8 paperback

ISBN-13: 978-1-4463-5561-9 e-pub
ISBN-10: 1-4463-5561-6 e-pub

ISBN-13: 978-1-4463-5560-2 PDF
ISBN-10: 1-4463-5560-8 PDF

Paperback edition printed in USA by RR Donnelley
for F&W Media International, LTD
Brunel House, Forde Close, Newton Abbot, TQ12 4PU, UK

10 9 8 7 6 5 4 3

Publisher Alison Myer
Acquisitions Editor Sarah Callard
Desk Editor Jeni Hennah
Project Editor Lin Clements
Design Manager Sarah Clark
Photographer Simon Whitmore
Production Manager Beverley Richardson

F+W Media Inc. publishes high quality books on a wide range of
subjects. For more great book ideas visit: **www.stitchcraftcreate.co.uk**